There's a Poet in Everyone

Dr. Diwakar Pokhriyal

Published by InkQuills Publishing House
www.inkquills.in

First Edition 2019

All Rights Reserved. Copyright © 2019

ISBN: 978-81-943552-0-5

The views and opinions expressed in this book are the author's own and the facts are as reported by them, and the publisher is not in any way liable for the same.

This book has been published in good faith that the work of the author is original. All efforts have been taken to make the material error-free. However, the publisher disclaims the responsibility.

This is a work of fiction. Names, Characters, Places and incidents are product of author's imagination. Any resemblance to any actual persons, living or dead, events or locales is entirely coincidental. No part of this publication may be reproduced, transmitted, or stored in a retrieval system, in any form or by any means, electronic, mechanical, photocopying, recording or otherwise, without the prior permission of the publisher.

DEDICATION

This book is dedicated to all poetry enthusiasts that want to learn more and want to live poetry.

This poetry book is dedicated to all those poets who write for the love of writing poetry.

ACKNOWLEDGEMENT

I want to thank my family for their blessings and support. I would also like to thank everyone who is associated with me through poetry and helped me in soaking the inspiration around. Every single appreciation of you fuels my passion towards writing poetry.

I also want to thank my photographer friend Ms. Payal Vohra for the beautiful book cover.

Poet's Corner

This book is to learn and enjoy poetry. Poetry is generally treated as something that is not important and needs minimal attention. Poetry has been limited to very few forms. Choice of any poet is his freedom, but the poet should first go through different forms of poetry. If the poet don't find any interest and fun, then he or she is free to choose any poetic form. I as a poet want poetry to become an integral part of our society; poetry should serve as a reason for something productive. Memorizing few concepts in rhyme or through an encryption is always a great way to learn things while using poetry.

My aim of writing this book is to introduce the poetry lovers to different forms of poetry. This to create a base among the poetry lovers to get a feel and understanding about poetry. Becoming a great poet is indeed a monumental task, but learning poetry is not. Anyone can learn poetry and enjoy it. I wish this book will help many aspiring poets to keep writing and enjoying poetry.

Writing poetry is always a fulfilling act and also sharing it with others. Through this book I am trying to share a small knowledge about poetry that can help the sparing poets.

I believe that "**There is a Poet in Everyone**" of us and we should enjoy that poet to the fullest.

"Keep Writing & Keep Shining"

Dr. Diwakar Pokhriyal

CONTENT

Chapter – 1 There is a Poet in everyone 1

Chapter – 2 ABC Poem 61

Chapter – 3 Acrostic Poetry 64

Chapter – 4 Abecedarian Poetry 66

Chapter – 5 Alliterative Poetry 69

Chapter – 6 Aquarian Poetry 71

Chapter – 7 Baccresieze Poetry 73

Chapter – 8 Cadence Poetry 75

Chapter – 9 Cinquian Butterfly Poetry 78

Chapter – 10 Cinquian 81

Chapter – 11 Couplets 82

Chapter – 12 Cromorna 85

Chapter – 13 Diagonal Acrostic 87

Chapter – 14 Double Acrostic 88

Chapter – 15 Duodara 91

Chapter – 16 Echo Verse 93

Chapter – 17 Enclosed Rhyme 95

Chapter – 18 Epitaphs 97

Chapter – 19 Etheree 99

Chapter – 20 Double Etheree 100

Chapter – 21 Etheree Reverse 102

Chapter – 22 Etheree Twin Double 104

Chapter – 23 Etheree Twin 109

Chapter – 24 English Ghazal 113

Chapter – 25 Fibonacci 115

Chapter – 26 Free Verse 117

Chapter – 27 Glosa 119

Chapter – 28 Golda Poetry 124

Chapter – 29 Haiku & Senryu 126

Chapter – 30 Lai Poetry 127

Chapter – 31 The Lyrette 128

Chapter – 32 The Marianne 131

Chapter – 33 Nonet 133

Chapter – 34 Quatrain 134

Chapter – 35 Quintet (English) 135

Chapter – 36 Rhyming 137

Chapter – 37 SESTINA Poetry 145

Chapter – 38 Streambed Quintet 149

Chapter – 39 Tetractys 151

Chapter – 40 The Kerf Poetry 152

Chapter – 41 Triplets 154

Chapter – 42 Tricubes Poetry 158

Chapter – 43 Treochair Poetry 160

Chapter – 44 Tanka 162

Chapter – 45 A Tritina 164

Chapter – 46 Villanelle Poetry 166

Chapter – 47 Yadu 168

Chapter – 48 A Zejel 170

Chapter – 49 Alphabet Fever Poetry 172

Chapter – 50 Freedoetry* (Freedom Poetry) 179

Chapter – 51 Poetry Rainbow 182

Chapter – 52 Heptaoem 186

Chapter – 53 Remix Poetry 188

Chapter – 54 Zig Zag Rhyming 200

Chapter – 55 Encryptive Poetry 201

Chapter – 1
There is a Poet in everyone

"I am very bad at poetry", I said.

"Oh! Is that so?", my friend smirked.

"Yes", I said.

"But it is so easy to learn poetry", he smiled.

"Obviously, for a poet like you it is, but for a normal human being like me, it is an impossible task", I was confident.

"No, There's a Poet in Everyone", my Friend said.

"What?", I was surprised listening to this.

"Ok, wait, you remember that poem twinkle-twinkle", he tried to test my memory.

"Wait, oh yes, that poem", I wrote.

"Twinkle, twinkle little star,
How I wonder what you are,
Up above the world so high,
Like a diamond in the sky"

"Great, now can you look at the last words of each line", he pointed.

"Yes, they are star, are, high and sky", I said.

"Yes, my wannabe poet, they are rhyming words", he said.

"What? Oh yes! The last two words sound similar and makes a rhyme", I observed.

"So now try something else?", he said.

"No, not now, let me understand how", I said.

"Yes, correct", he laughed.

"I said a sentence", I was surprised.

"Break this sentence into two lines", he said.

"No, not now, let me understand how".

"Oh! Wow!", I exclaimed.

"Yes, this will also rhyme with how and now", he again laughed.

"Yes", I joined him.

"Congratulations! You have become a poet", he patted my back.

"So soon?", I said.

"You have created a two-line rhyming couplet", he said.

"What?", I was feeling happy as well as surprised.

"Yes, two means couple and rhyming lines means rhyming couplet", he said and I was amazed.

"It's not so difficult", I was enjoying the creative process.

"So let's learn more", he said and I nodded my head.

"Write a poem on any sports you like keeping each alphabet of the title as first alphabet of each line", I said.

"What?", I was confused and he started reciting something.

What?

(Acrostic)

"Why so confuse?,

Hope is the key,

Amidst the dark clouds,

Timeless happiness awaits"

"The title of this poem is "What?" and you can see that first alphabet of the title is the first alphabet of the first line. Similarly, the second alphabet of the title will become the first alphabet of second line and so on. The order should not be changed", he explained.

"This is interesting", I said and tried writing a poem.

Easy

(Acrostic)

Energy can be easily wasted,

And time will also fly away,

Slow and steady might lose,

Yes, the focus is the key.

"Yes, perfect", my friend said and I was happy about learning another poetry form.

"There is abc poetry where you use four alphabets in a row as first alphabet of each line and the first alphabet of last line can be any. There is another version of it in which you make a poem such that every word comes in the alphabetical order", he showed his poems.

Smiling heart

(ABC poetry)

Are you so independent, that

Blinders of mind can't flaunt you,

Colonial cousins of disaster may create upheaval,

Death will never become defunct,

Still posses that smiling heart.

Young Enthusiasm
(ABC poetry)
A Baked Cake,
Delicious enough,
For Generating Haste,
Instigate Jerks Knowingly,
Leaving Man Nasty,
Outside Placid Quantum,
Reinforce Subtle Treasury,
Unknown Venom Wears,
Xeric Youthful Zest

"Oh! This is easy, I can write one", I said and wrote one.
"Yes, this is cool. See, you are learning fast Mr. Poet", he smiled looking at me.
"Oh, this is unbelievable! I am becoming a poet?", I was excited.
"And a bigger version of this is Abecedarian Poetry, in this poetry form each line starts with the alphabet in alphabetical order", he tried.
"That means, the poem have 26 lines?", I imagined.
"Yes, and rhyme is not necessary", I said and he started writing a poem.

Depression
(Abecedarian Poetry)
Alas! I have lost,

There's a Poet in Everyone

Brutally, from thyself,

Ceasing to exist, now,

Duped determination

Erratic behaviour,

False belief,

Grinding thy soul,

Have faith, Oh Man!,

In the Almighty,

Just at the corner,

Kind heart and soul exists,

Lust can't win,

Moans are momentary,

Nasty clouds will fade away,

Oh, I can listen to you,

Purging my dejection,

Quitting my tale,

Rising pain, no purpose,

Slowly and steadily,

Time is ticking away,

Unity isn't an option,

Venom has acted fast,

Wishes are out of the box,

Xeroxing my erroneous fate,

Yes, I am about to sleep,

Zooming into the depressive valley.

"Perfect", he said and I was happy.

"Can you repeat words with same starting alphabets?", he questioned.

"Means? Apple and Aeroplane?", I spoke.

"Yes, apple and airplanes can be a line of a poem and if others lines also contain such words with repeating starting alphabets then it would be called as Alliteration (repetitiveness). Rhyming is optional. Such poems are called alliterative poems.", he showed an example.

Wait

(Alliterative poetry)

Waiting wisely, having water,
For my friend, foe and fire,
Tickling time talking to me,
New night has nasty desires,
Life limps legitimately,
Thoughts thwarted by time,
Alone at artist's adobe,
Blank board of brine,
A time will come,
When warning woes will vanish,
Mind will maintain my dignity,
Brutal brain of battle will replenish.

"Wow, what an articulate repetition of alphabets", I was amazed at this.

"Oh! I forgot, two rhyming lines are called couplet, three triplets, and four quatrains", he told me.

"I will write this time", I started scribbling.

Love

(Couplet)

A glimpse of your eyes,

Is fresh as the skies.

Love

(Triplet)

A glimpse of your eyes,

Is fresh as the skies,

Makes me wonder about our ties.

Learning

(Quatrain)

It will stay with me,

Like my parents forever,

It will make me free,

It will make me clever.

"Brother, these are spot on, congratulations on becoming a poet", My friend tapped my shoulder.

"What? No? So easily?", I was stunned.

"Yes, you got the sense of creating a poem. Now putting experience, meanings and more things into it will come through practice of writing again and again", I had a glass of water.

"I want to learn more forms?", I said.

"How many?", he laughed.

"I want to hit a half century", I emulate a classic cover drive.

"Are you sure?", he tried to test my patience.

"You can lock it brother", I smiled.

"Ok then let's move ahead", he said and I was excited.

"For an acrostic poem, if you use the same alphabet in same numeric order as in the title, then it will become diagonal acrostic", he completed and looked at me, I was blank.

"I mean, first alphabet of title as first alphabet of the first word of the first line. Then second alphabet of the title will be the first alphabet of the second word in the second line and so on.", he said.

"Oh, kind of a diagonal, if we see the alphabets of title in the poem", I tried to imagine.

"Yes, true", he wrote a poem.

Yes

(Diagonal acrostic)

Yawning at me,

The epic response,

Lethargic and stupid kid.

"What could be then double acrostic?", he questioned.

"Double acrostic? Repeating the alphabets twice or in two different lines", I tried.

"No, you have to keep the basic nature of an acrostic intact", he gave a clue.

"First two words of each line related to the title", I again tried.

"Kinda close you are, the first and last alphabet of each line corresponds to the title", he said and I understood.

"Oh, wait, I will write one", I started writing.

Lie

(Acrostic)

Life is lethargic and frail,

Instantaneous emotional 'I'

Enough warriors needed for the spree.

"Oh Mr. Poet is on the spot", he said and I closed my notebook.

"I am feeling hungry", I said and he laughed.

"Ok, let's have a sandwich", he went inside the kitchen.

"Thank you", I said having one.

"You know there is a poetry in this also", he giggled.

"What? A sandwich poetry", I said and we both laughed.

"No, what do we call when something is between two surfaces", He asked.

"Enclosed?", I figured it out.

"Yes, enclosed rhyme", he finished his sandwich.

"So what might be an enclosed rhyme?", he asked.

"Got it, when one rhyme is sandwiched between other", I figured it out.

"Amazing Mr. Poet. So write a poem for both (Rhyme and Enclosed Rhyme)", he signaled and I started writing.

Epic
(Rhyming Poem)

The one who stands alone,
Changes no tone,
Is the one who rises,
Winning all the prizes,

Breaking the rules,
His own thoughts, his own schools,
He will extinguish the sun,
Leaving the world stun,

Yes, he is the epic one,
Requires no gun,
Determined and passionate,
Having the key of every gate.

Searching my love
(Enclosed Rhyme)

In this world so bright,
I am searching my love,

There's a Poet in Everyone

Flying like a dove,
All through day and night,

Hope is what I have within,
Timeless efforts are required,
Is the right person I hired?
Chances looks so thin.

"Wow, these are good", my friend applauded and I felt confident.
"I am liking it", I was enjoying.
"What if I'll not rhyme?", I said with curiosity.
"Not a problem, then it would be a free verse poetry", My friend said.
"Really?", I laughed.
"Yes", he smiled and showed a poem to me.

Child's play
(Free Verse)
Raining efforts at will,
Crossing the road of sanity,
Life takes a halt,
To check on the heart,
And the determination,
As, crafting a sky,
With umpteen stars,
And a moon,
Isn't a child's play,

"Wow, that's great?", I enjoyed the poem.

"Have you ever visited a graveyard?", my friend asked.

"Yes, I also saw something written there, 2-3 lines", I tried to recollect.

"That's an epitaph", he pointed.

"Oh, is the so?", I thought.

"Yo", he looked at me and laughed.

"So, an epitaph is a few lines written in the honor of the deceased person on its tomb", he said.

"That means somebody else writes it for the person who dies", I had a doubt.

"The person can always willingly say before his death about what should be written after his death", my friend cleared my doubt.

"Okay, I shall try one", I started scribbling.

Epitaph

I learned with time,

Life is a rhyme,

If you think otherwise,

You are committing a crime.

"Oh, Mr. Poet", he clapped.

"Thank you, thank you", I was feeling ecstatic.

"Is There any poem you like; I mean from well-known poet?", he asked.

"Yes", I started remembering a few.

There's a Poet in Everyone

"Can you tell me four lines out of any poem you like", he said and I told him a few lines.

In a few minutes he wrote something a showed it to me.

Glosa- 1

First four Lines taken from Sarojini Naidu's poem - 'Autumn Song'

Like a joy on the heart of a sorrow,
The sunset hangs on a cloud;
A golden storm of glittering sheaves,
Of fair and frail and fluttering leaves,

Temptations and reality of the life,
Unmatched and untouched,
Misunderstood sanity, blind faith,
Humanity has lost the touch,
Roads are full, but hearts are empty,
Tears are waived off of emotion,
Only money and money rules,
No shoulder to cry on,
But we want to see the moon in elation,
Like a joy on the heart of a sorrow,

The leaves fall off with a smile,
Oh! You forgot my love,

Dr. Diwakar Pokhriyal

The timeless demon that kills,

The timeless sighs that tears apart,

And in the pain that is eternal,

The smile is just a mask,

A mask that makes you happy,

For an instant and then leaves,

Like a night, and to complete a task,

The sunset hangs on a cloud;

Yet, I know this loneliness,

Can still bring me the strength,

The positivity to survive,

In this world of black magic,

In this world of tragedies,

In this world of satire,

A ray of hope climbs,

The mountain of blemishes,

Like a tornado of burning fire,

A golden storm of glittering sheaves,

So, it's time to rethink,

And dive into the silent valley,

The pearl is somewhere inside,

It's time we should understand,

The filth we are painting,

It's time we should disperse,

There's a Poet in Everyone

To re-unite at the dawn,
And I love this thought,
And I love this pretty universe,
Of fair and frail and fluttering leaves.

"My god! What is this?", I was surprised at this.
"This is a GLOSA, a poetry form where you take four lines from any poem you like, write in on the top and then add four stanzas of 10 lines each to it. The last line of each stanza is the line from the first four lines", he said and it took me some time to soak it up.
"Got it Mr. Poet?", my friend was looking at me.
"That means we can take four lines from any poem and then use these lines as the last line of each stanza, meaning the first line of those four lines will be the last line of first ten-line stanza, second line of the first four lines will be the last line of second ten-line stanza and so on", I asked.
"Yes, you are absolutely right and then there is one more such long form of poem, that is called Sestina", he patted my back.
"Sestina? Is this a dance form?", I started dancing.
"Yes, it makes your brain dance while constructing the rhyme", he laughed.
"Constructing rhyme?", I was thrilled.
"Yes, in this form of poetry you choose 6 words that don't rhyme with each other. The poem consists of six paragraphs of six lines each and there is a pattern for the usage of the words", my friend started writing some numbers on the white board.

"Wow, numbers and English?", I was amazed.

"Look at these numbers 123456, 615243, 364125, 532614, 451362 and 246531. These are the orders in which the words will come into the poem. And there will be last three lines after these six stanzas, the three lines together are called an envoy where in each line two words out of six chosen would come and the order would be 25-43-61. In the first line of an envoy, the second word can come anywhere, but the fifth word will come at the end of the first line", he told me and I was fully confused now.

"Okay, look at this example", he said and I started reading a long poem.

Against the Order
(A Sestina)

Look at this slip,
Let me throw this on fire,
You murky teen,
You need to train,
Your brain, life is rough,
Will you stand the test?

What the hell is this Test?
I'll never slip,
The road is not rough,
I have in me the fire,
Go catch your train,

There's a Poet in Everyone

I am the power, I am the teen,

Yes, you careless teen,
You can't pass this test,
You should catch a train,
Get lost, you will slip,
And burn in fire,
Your life will be rough,

My life would be rough?
I am a powerful teen,
I possess within, a fire,
A fire burning, need a test?
I will stand tall after every slip,
You can't understand, go catch a train,

Ha ha ha, catch a train?
You are a loser, becoming rough,
I am sure you will slip,
You are overconfident, frail teen,
You can't even stand a chance in a test,
And you talk about the fire?

Yes, I am the fire,
I can train,
My brain will clear the test,

Dr. Diwakar Pokhriyal

I will win, no matter how rough,

I am the power, I am the teen,

You can't bring me down, you can only watch, if I'll slip.

The fire kept burning and life became rough,

The train was off track, for both adult and teen,

Who shall pass this test? Or both will slip?

"Oh, a clear example", I fully understood.

"You like vanilla ice cream?", he said and passed on the ice cream.

"Is there a poetry form, on vanilla?", I laughed.

"There is a Villanelle poetry form. In this form we use two refrains and two repeating rhymes. This a nineteen lines poem. The structure of this poem is A1bA2 – abA1 – abA2 - abA1 - abA2 – abA1A2, where A1 and A2 are two refrains, the a & b are two repeating rhymes", my friend said and left me to try my hand this form.

"This is hard", I said.

"Ok, Mr. Poet this is your homework and wait, there is a short form of Sestina which is known as a tritina. In tritina poem there are three words, three triplets and an envoy. The order is 123, 321, 132 and an envoy is a single line consisting all three words 123", he said and I left the place.

The next day I went to my friend's house again.

"Here are the poems", I showed him.

The Park

(Villanelle Poetry)

In the night so dark,

I set to find the peace,

I sat on the park,

That was so stark,

I was feeling at the crease,

In the night so dark,

In search of a spark,

I found a piece,

I sat on the park,

Suddenly heard a bark,

And voices of trees,

In the night so dark,

New journey I had to embark,

As if I had to pay the fees,

I sat on the park,

Found not even a mark,

Hiding from the bees,

In the night so dark,

I sat on the park.

Decision to play
(A tritina)

In a sweet, touching day,
I was out to play,
Oh Gosh! I lost my way,

This is not the way,
I was supposed to open the day,
With a fantabulous play,

But Alas! No trace of my play,
I couldn't find my way,
What an unfortunate day,

But I will change this day when I will play after finding my way.

"Do you know what are the syllables?", my friend asked.
"Syllable? No idea?", I said.
"So, get idea", he said.
"What?", I looked at him, he was laughing.
"My mobile network is good", I said.
"Syllable is a segment of speech which is uninterrupted and consisting of a vowel sound. The vowel might or might not precede or follow consonant sounds", he said.
"Need an example", I said.
"Ok, can you spell the word 'eye'", he asked.

"Yes, EYE", I spelled.
"Have you experienced any break while the pronunciation?", he asked.
"No, I can even replace this as 'I'", I said.
"Exactly, the syllable count of this word is one", my friend said.
"Oh ok", I said.
"What about the word syllable?", I asked.
"Syl-la-ble, three syllables", I said and he nodded his head.
"So, you got the idea?", he again confirmed.
"Yes, somewhat", I was still not confident.
"Okay then, tell me the syllable count in each line of this poem", he said and gave me a poem.

Amazed

(Aquarian)

Oh Lord!

I am amazed,

Looking at the blindness,

Of heart.

"Two syllable in first line, four syllables in second line, six syllables in the third line and again two syllables in the last line", I said.
"Can you explain a bit?", my friend was still not convinced.
"Oh, lord, I, am, at, the, of and heart is having one syllable each, as each word is continuous in speech with one vowel. Oh the other hand amazed can be spelled as a-mazed which means, a is one syllable and then 'mazed' is pronounced as one which means this is one syllable.

Same goes with blindness as it can be broken into blind-ness and hence two syllables", I said in a firm voice.

"Wow! Spot on", my friend was impressed.

"So, let's dive into the sea of poetry that contains syllables", my friend said.

"Yes, let's go", I said.

"The previous example that I gave you was 'Aquarian' poetry consisting of four lines with 2-4-6-2 syllables each line", he pointed out.

"Oh, okay", I noted.

"Next poetry form is Baccresieze", he said.

"What?", I laughed hearing the name.

"Baccresieze poetry is the poetry forms that consist of three quatrains, the first three lines of each quatrain consists of 8 syllables and the last line of each quatrain consist of 4 syllables each. The rhyme scheme is AaxB bxAB xxxB, x means no rhyme".

"What is the difference between A and a?", I asked.

"A & B means same lines would be repeated and a, b mean words rhyming with A & B", he told me.

"Oh, let me try", I said and wrote a poem in some time.

Her sacrifice
(Baccresieze poetry)
She lived her life, only for love
She hugged the strife, only for love,
Like a prince, he was raised by her,

There's a Poet in Everyone

Her sacrifice.

Imagination was all nice,
But reality knocked one day,
She lived her life, only for love
Her sacrifice

The lousy face of prince emerged,
Abandoning purity, bliss,
The time cried, humanity died,
Her sacrifice.

"Very good, can you find the rhyme scheme and syllable structure in the poem above?", my friend challenged.
"Give me some time", I started observing the poem.
"Yes, I'll be back in two minutes", my friend went to the other room.

He came back in next 5 minutes.

"So, Mr. Poet, need some assistance?", he started mocking me.
"First three lines of each quatrain consist of eight syllables and last repeating line consist four syllables. Last four syllables of the first line are repeated as last four syllables of a second line in first quatrain only. First line of first quatrain is repeated as the third line of second quatrain. The rhyme scheme is AaxB BxAB xxxB, where x means there is no rhyme", I completed and he clapped.

"Cadence is another poetry form where the syllable count is 1-2-3-4-4-8-5 per line. There is no rhyme in the poem and the lines should end with strong words. Cadence is often related to music with rising and falling of voices", he showed an example.

Eureka
(Cadence)
Great,
Brilliant,
Eureka,
An idea
Pure energy,
To drastically change the course
Of known history

"Great. What is that?", I look at a painting.
"Butterfly", he laughed.
"Is there a poetry related to butterfly?", I said in a jolly tone.
"Yes", he laughed.
"What?", I was surprised.
"There is cinquian poetry and the other form is butterfly cinquian, but we will start with three lines poetry first", my friend staring writing something in the board.
"Yes, that would be great", I was excited.
"Haiku and Senryu are Japanese forms of poetry. Haiku is a three-line poem with syllable count of 5-7-5 and it should have a seasonal

reference. There is no rhyme in this form. If you replicate the same structure in another poem dealing with emotions, it would be a Senryu. There should be a turn of thoughts in the second line or somewhere in between", he completed.

"Oh! So the only difference between these two forms is the seasonal reference?", I tried to clear my doubt.

"Yes, true", he showed me the examples.

Childhood
(Haiku)

Spring of stars around,

Childhood reminiscences,

The night becomes day.

Wish
(Senryu)

Your Tranquility,

Oxygen of my terrain,

A wishful thinking

"It takes some courage to attempt this form", I was amazed.

"Yes, a lot of courage. Similarly, if you add two more lines of in the poem above it will become a Tanka. Tanka is a poetry form consisting of five lines with no rhyme and the syllable count of 5-7-5-7-7".

He wrote a poem on the spot.

Perspective
(Tanka)

Just out of the blue,

A Scintillating glory

Or tragedy rule,

Life is biased, is unfair,

Meaningful or a decoy

"Beautiful it is", I could feel the flow.
"So now coming to five line poems, tetractys is another interesting form. Rhyming is not required in this form and the syllable count is 1-2-3-4-10", he completed and I started writing.
"Wait, I'll write one", I said and he smiled.

Love
(Tetractys)

Look,

Deep down,

Into my soul,

And find your love,

Shaping my thoughts, shaping my desires.

"This is perfect. Do you remember quintet?", he asked.
"No, I remember quatrain that is a poem of four lines", I tried to remember.

"Oh, quintet is a poem having five lines and rhyme scheme of ababb. There is no syllable count, few believe that it follows an iambic pentameter, but that's optional. You can extend the five line stanzas to any number. So, if you will write three stanzas then the rhyme scheme would be ababb, cdcdd, efeff and so on. Streambed quintet is a quintet having a syllable count of 7-4-5-3-5, rest all rules are similar as the quintet", he finished his line.

"Okay, this seems interesting", I wrote two poems.

Waiting for love
(Quintet)

I held your hands my love,

In pursuit of freshness and care,

You flew away like a dove,

Reflecting deepest fear of share,

Never thought, Oh love! How could I dare,

You are my love so pure,

Every touch of yours instills life,

You are my penultimate cure,

 Above my every single strife,

But oh love, you killed my hope with a knife.

Yet love knows no barrier,

I am still breathing in your wait,

You are my only carrier,

Towards that heaven's gate,

I am waiting, please come back Oh mate!

Battle
(Streambed Quintet)

Alas! This world is now hell,

Soul wants to yell,

Prepare for the war,

Kill the scar,

Only win to smell.

Decide your destiny now,

No matter how,

Dig down deep inside,

With the pride,

Perfect time is now.

"Yes, Mr. Poet you are learning very fast", my friend grinned.

"I am enjoying the poems and the structures. This is so fun and an exercise for the brain", I said.

"So, let's do some more exercise. Cinquian is also a poem of five lines, no rhyme and the syllable count is 2-4-6-8-2. Butterfly cinquian is another form with nine lines. It has the syllable count of 2-4-6-8-2-4-6-8-2 and no rhyming", he showed me poems of both the forms.

"Okay, is this butterfly shape (when the poem is centered) the reason for the name", I asked with curiosity.

There's a Poet in Everyone

"Yes it is", he smiled.

"Great", I picked up the pen again.

Faith
(Cinquian)

Trust me,

When I hug tight,

And kiss you in the rain,

The moments dissolve into me,

Like you.

Power
(Cinquian Butterfly)

Power,

Is absolute,

It converts a human,

Either into a bloody beast,

Hungry,

Or into resilient saint,

What is your destiny?

That can be seen,

Clearly.

"Etheree is another poetry form which follows a syllabic pattern of 1-2-3-4-5-6-7-8-9-10, rhyming can be there or can't be", he showcased one of his best poem.

Dr. Diwakar Pokhriyal

Masked Freedom

(Etheree)

High,

On beer,

Feeling proud,

And ecstatic,

Forgetting the truth,

Forgetting existence

Forgetting self, is one way,

To prepare self to run away

To prepare self for devastation,

Masked as enjoyment and freedom in life.

"What if I reverse it?", I said jokingly.

"It will become a reverse etheree", he laughed.

"That means, the syllable count will become 10-9-8-7-6-5-4-3-2-1?", I asked in surprise.

"Yes", He was in no mood to stop.

"What if I will add one etheree and one reverse ethree?", I tried to make fun.

"It will become a double etheree with a syllable count of 1-2-3-4-5-6-7-8-9-10-10-9-8-7-6-5-4-3-2-1", he said.

"What if I will add rhyming lines with each line of double etheree", I was trying to troll him.

"Then it will become a twin double etheree", he shook his head.

"What the hell? This is insane! That means a poetry form with the syllable count of 1-1-2-2-3-3-4-4-5-5-6-6-7-7-8-8-9-9-10-10-10-10-9-9-8-8-7-7-6-6-5-5-4-4-3-3-2-2-1-1. How can someone write such a long poem and that too with a syllable structure?", I was shocked.

"That's why few poets believe that syllable count kills a poem", he said.

"This is really amazing", I was still thinking about that form.

"And if you rhyme lines only for first 10 lines then it will become a twin etheree. The syllable count is 1-1-2-2-3-3-4-4-5-5-6-6-7-7-8-8-9-9-10-10".

"Wonderful this is", I said and looked at his notes.

Realization,
(Etheree Double)

I,

Woke up,

To find out,

Hidden treasure,

In the shining sun

In the dancing droplets,

In the shades of lovely trees,

In the chills of flowing wind,

In the chirping of freedom around,

When suddenly I heard a voice, Alas!

Realization of crude emotions,

Realization of emptiness,

Dr. Diwakar Pokhriyal

Realization of the pain,

Realization of hate,

Realization of,

Realization,

I slept again,

In hope of,

A new,

Life.

War of Aggression
(Etheree Reverse)

Sparkling eyes were hypnotized to kill truth,

To rule the empire of dissonance,

To craft an era of freedom,

I crawled into aggression,

In the end of the war,

I lost my desires,

And my passion,

And my Hope,

My life,

Me

Unity
(Etheree Twin Double)

We,

See,

There's a Poet in Everyone

Just I,

Lone thy,

Loses fun,

Love gets stun,

Unity just rocks,

Fixes all blocks

Teamwork always glow,

No matter how slow,

Aloofness kills slowly

Company is holy

Let's unite to fill the gap,

A shower under same tap,

We are just born to love and care,

Playing jointly with equal share

Under the sky of serenity,

Inside deep blue sea of dignity

A layer of firm trust lies there anew,

Understood by true souls which are left few,

Dr. Diwakar Pokhriyal

A time to spread this important message,

Driving this sleeping and empty carriage,

It's time, wake up for agility,

Now silently kill humility

The beautiful flower of hope,

With fragrance of truth without dope

Swimming in sea of passion,

Without fear of recession

Flirting with naughty fate,

As if opening gate,

Gate of real trust,

Where love enter "must"

Finding true friends

Changing old trends

Purity,

Unity,

Sees right,

No fight,

There's a Poet in Everyone

We,

Flee.

My love

(Twin Etheree)

Sweet,

Greet,

Leaves me,

In glee,

Lovely wish,

Or nice dish,

A smile of you,

Leaves without clue,

Like the wind so swift,

As a precious gift,

Like a touch of fingers,

Where only love lingers,

You are here so merciful,

An angel so beautiful,

Dr. Diwakar Pokhriyal

A touchy shower for my soul
You are only romantic goal,

Instigating care and trust inside,
For taking an everlasting stride,

Resting inside continuous hear beat,
You are "My Love", so cute, bubbly and sweet.

"I am spell bound", I said.
"Mr. Poet, if you will remove the first line from reverse etheree, then it will become a Nonet poem", he signaled.
"Nine-line poetry, with no rhyme scheme and a syllable count of 9-8-7-6-5-4-3-2-1", I said and he nodded his head in yes.

Waste
(Nonet)
This,
Lone world,
Speaks aloud,
Trying to grab,
The life out of death,
Instead, finds emptiness,
Darkness under burning sun,
Haziness shining all around,
Misunderstands the whole true meaning.

"Wow", I was amazed.

"Cromorna is a poem of 12 lines; the rhyme scheme is abab cbcb dbdb and syllable count is 5-3-5-3-5-3-5-3-5-3-5-3", he looked at my face which was shining with happiness, the happiness of becoming a poet. "I'll write one", I wrote in another fifteen minutes.

Lesson
(Cromorna)

Spring in the summer,

With fire,

A quest for glimmer,

With desire,

Life is vehicle,

You, tyre,

For Happy cycle,

A buyer,

They will only share,

An attire,

And who am I here?

A liar.

"Do you like mathematics?", he asked.

"Poetry and mathematics?", my exclamation marks were vanishing second by second.

"Yes, you remember Fibonacci series?", he tried to check my memory. "I do remember, it goes like this 1-1-2-3-5-8 and so on. Basically the first number is 1 and the next line is the sum of the above two lines. It can be seen as this:

1,

1,

2 (1+1, sum of above two numbers),

3 (2+1, sum of above two numbers),

5 (3+2, sum of above two numbers),

8 (5+3. The sum of above two numbers) and so on", I completed.

"Perfect, so if you make this series as a syllable count of each line and make rhyming optional then it will become a Fibonacci poem", he pointed out and I was still in awe.

Zest
(Fibonacci)

Have,

Zest,

To rise,

Against odds,

To pounce and bounce, to,

Cement emphatic legacy,

Which is born out of sheer determination to win

There's a Poet in Everyone

"Have you ever been to mountains?", my friend asked.

"Yes, is there a poetry form on this too", I looked at him in disbelief.

"You know the phenomenon of Echo?", he asked.

"Yes, the sound coming back to us", I told him.

"Echo verse is a poetry form based on this. Every alternate line reflects the echo of the last or the last two syllables of previous line", he showed me a poem.

End

Control your uncanny surge,

Urge,

Good and bad can't merge,

Urge,

Oh Boy, fanatically you have to diverge,

Urge

Consider it as reality or as hormonal,

Zonal,

Now weeds cannot converge

Urge,

Stop praying for profound spring

Ring

Even saints are now fanatical and selfish,

Fish

No time for you to pretend

End

Misbehavior you should only attend

End

Nothing in this lifeless world you can amend

End

Forget to paint a phoenix or a trend

End

All the wall are broken you can't mend,

End

Your hands are fiercely broken you can't lend

End

Iterations of desires knows no bend

End

Oh my noxious human you have reached the dead end

End

"This is really a fun", I enjoyed the form.

"Duodora is another form which contains two septets (stanza of seven lines), the syllable count is 4-6-5-5-5-10-10-4-6-5-5-5-10-10 and the rhyme scheme in this poem is Axxxxxb Axxxxxb", my friend drew the structure.

"So, the first line of each septet is same?", I asked.

"Yes", he showed me a poem.

Never Pretend
(Duodora)

Never Pretend,

To be correct or wrong,

There's a Poet in Everyone

Life is a full circle

Swinging pendulum

An unknown darkness,

And also an enlightening journey,

Who knows at which quadrant you will die,

Never Pretend,

To go into the books

Of trust and friendship,

Of pure emotions,

Of goodness and hope

Without having a wholesome human heart,

Because if you are then it is a lie

"Lyrette and Marianne are other two interesting forms of poetry. Lyrette consists of seven lines, it is unrhymed and each line should end with a strong word (means no prepositions), the syllable count is 2-3-4-5-4-3-2", he took a breath.

"Ok", I said.

"Marianne is a five lines poem with syllable pattern of 4-6-8-4-2 per line and the rhyming scheme is axaxa, where x means unrhymed. The poem is centered and titled", he wrote both poems in from of me.

Sense
(Lyrette)
Nonsense,

Dr. Diwakar Pokhriyal

Is this world,

That fights for truth,

Misunderstanding,

Meaning of peace,

Pays the price,

With life.

Wings
(Marianne)

I have those wings,

For the humanity,

Wings of desire, fire and swings,

Let that lone sweet,

Bell rings

"Is there any inclined rhyme?", I just asked out of curiosity.
"Yadu is a Burmese form of poetry. The rhyme in it is not the inclined, but climbing rhyme. It consists of three stanzas of five lines each. The first four lines of each stanza have a syllable count of four and last line of each stanza can have 5,7,9 or 11 syllables. Like the haiku, it also must have a seasonal reference".

Angel and Devil
(Yadu Poetry)

Silent chaste smile,

Opens file bit slow,

There's a Poet in Everyone

Agile is heart,

Hide in shirt, now,

Like flying in passion, tied with compassion

Hot summer burns,

A Truth churns on,

None learns to care,

Shy to share life,

Lose layers of the true feelings

Both dives deep,

Like a sleeping

And creeping dive,

Short beehive bleeds,

A stride of honey blood totally insane.

"Wow! This is great, Mr. Poet", he loved it.

"Thank you so much", I was ecstatic.

"Golda is another poetry form in which the title is mandatory. It consists of 12 lines and the syllable counts is 2-2-4-1-4-2-2-1-2-4-4-2. The rhyme scheme is xxxxxaxxxxxa", he said and wrote a poem.

Waiting

(Golda Poetry)

A glimpse,

Of you,

Dr. Diwakar Pokhriyal

Keeps me alive,

In,

This rotten world

Oh love,

The sighs,

Weeps,

Often,

Fearing of death,

When we fly high,

Like dove.

"Yes, this is good. I liked it", I said.

"So then, two more forms of poetry from my side. One is kerf and another is Zejel, Zejel is a poetry form in which you can write any number of quatrains. You have to start with a triplet (three line) and then follow it up with the quatrains (four lines). The triplet should be rhyming and the last line of each quatrain should rhyme with the triplet, the rhyme scheme will become aaa-bbba- ccca-ddda etc. Each line has the syllable count of eight", he stopped and started drinking some water.

"Ok, what about Kerf?", I was anxious to know.

"Mr. Poet, Kerf consist of four tercets (triplets that doesn't rhyme). It follows the rhyme scheme of abc-abc-dec-dec and the syllable count for each tercet is 6-7-10 and hence the syllable count for the whole poem is 6-7-10-6-7-10-6-7-10-6-7-10", he gave me his book and I started reading both poems.

Comparison
(Zejel poetry)

Look at the monk, walking lone,
And poor me having no dial tone,
Engulfed completely by the loan,

I looked around, Goon was behind,
Including me, whole world is blind,
Everyone ahead, me rewind,
Feeling now, as if I am thrown,

And that lone monk wanders in peace,
Poor me, ambitious to touch Greece,
Not able to earn the damn fees,
My mom says 'Your brain has been grown?'

Find a way
(Kerf Poetry)

Oh my! I am livid,
Where are my empty plates?
I am poor by mind not by my actions,

But flaw is the cupid,
That can turn around our fates,
Just we have to keep checking reactions,

Dr. Diwakar Pokhriyal

Lacking food might turn bad,

Forcing innocents to lie,

Who will save these chaste ballast emotions?

Let us not become sad,

Let us find something to tie

To move together in worst rejections

"Mr. Poet, you have learnt more than 40 forms of poetry", my friend giggled.

"What?", I was in disbelief and I again started checking my notebook.

"You don't believe in your teacher", he laughed.

"Oh my god! It's really more than 40 poetry forms", I was amazed looking at this.

"You want to learn more?", my friend looked at me.

"Of Course yes", I smiled.

"Ok then I give you a free hand", my friend laughed.

"Free Hand?", I was surprised.

"Yes, lets write a Tricube poetry", he said.

"Tricube? Is it related to cube we read in Mathematics?", I asked while thinking about mathematics.

"Yes Mr poet, in this form you will write total nine lines, there will be three stanzas and every stanza will have 3 lines and every live will have 3 syllables", he stooped and had a sip of water.

"What a great thought, I am so surprised that people think so much?", I said and started trying one.

Lost Way
(Tricube Poetry)

I have read,

Till my death,

All known books,

But never,

Ever tried

To read self,

And so lost,

My own way,

When alive.

"Yes exactly this is it", my friend said and I was happy.
"Try another one, this is called Treochair poetry, in this form there can be variable number of tercets", he said.
"Tercets means three lines right?", I was trying to recall.
"Yes, and the first line of tercet will have 3 syllables, second will have 7 and third will also have 7 syllables. There will be a lot of alliteration and in terms of rhyme scheme, the first line of each tercet shall rhyme with the third one", he showed me an example.

Tell a tale
(Trochair poetry)

Tell a tale,

Dr. Diwakar Pokhriyal

To the minds and to the hearts

They can stand or swiftly sail

Let them see,

Beyond the normal eyes,

Experience the silent sea,

Male, Female,

They are all equivalent

To embrace them, tell a tale

"Oh! This is amazing", I was ecstatic.

"One last form from my side for today is Lai Poetry".

"Lai?", the name amazed me a bit.

"Yes Lai poetry is French poetry and it consists of 9 lines. The rhyme scheme for the nine lines are as follows aabaabaab", he said.

"Does that mean I have to use only two rhymes in whole poem?", I asked.

"Yes true and the syllable count would be 5 for a rhyming lines and 2 for the rhyming lines", he said.

"OK, wait let me try one", I said and tried writing one.

Just see
(Lai Poetry)

Do trust your own feel,

Do check your own deal,

There's a Poet in Everyone

Trust me,

Wins you have to seal,

Perfection is reel,

Just me,

Only thing to steal

In a day, a meal,

Just see.

"Oh my God! You have become such an amazing poet", he said reading my poem.

"Is it so?", I was so happy.

"I love hindi and urdu Ghazal, is there any such poetry form in English?", I asked.

"Yes there is and have same rules as for hindi or urdu one. Means you have to start with a rhyming couplet and then follow by other coulplets in which the second line rhymes with the first couplet. In the last couplet you use the sign of a poet or something of that sort", he said and I smiled.

"Will it be like this?", I just recited one to him.

Afterlife
(English Ghazal)

I experienced life, in the midst of chaos

I have trusted a knife, in the midst of chaos

I cannot pick up the stars, walking on this earth,

Dr. Diwakar Pokhriyal

So I entrusted the strife, in the midst of chaos,

Lost inside the blankness of colorful desires,
I Looked solace as wife, in the midst of chaos,

Such emotional tremors hit me so often,
This silent night looks rife, in the midst of chaos,

Walking with melancholy thought 'Oh My Dear friend'
Thinking what's afterlife, in the midst of chaos.

"Yes this is perfect, now you have got the sense of writing poetry", my friend was so happy.
"It's all because of you", I said
"And that's all from my side", he smiled and I left the place after having some more talks.

I was feeling amazing. In the next two months I practiced a lot and often visited my friend for guidance. I also kept on reading different forms of poetry on the internet. It was an amazing time for me, I learned a lot and I enjoyed a lot. In the next few months I thought of experimenting with poetry forms on my own and came with some amazing idea's. I wondered if so many aspiring poets will start to experiment on their own after going through an existing form then how much richer we will become. I started writing the experimental forms of poetry. My friend came to know about this and he came running to me.

"So Mr Poet, now it is your turn to be a teacher", he said and I started laughing.

"Alphabetic Fever poetry is an insane form of poetry with no syllable count, no line limits and no rhyme scheme, but you have to start every word with the same alphabet", I said and his eyes got welled up.

"Wow, alliteration to its extreme", he was impressed.

"Yes, very true", I said and showed him my poem written in my notebook.

Erroneously Enacted
(The Alphabet Fever poetry)
Elephant elopes effortlessly,
Evidences emit Excuses
Emergent Eyes erode,
Emphatic epical epic,
Entertaining eagle-eous eagerness,
Emitting entrant energy,
Envisioning embarking emergence,
Encapsulating enticing exactness,
Ever-ready errant enchants,
Engulfing eroding emptiness,
Ears elude enlightenment,
Engendering ebb,

Endangered eclipses evolving

Erroneous errors,

Edgy eggs experience,

Emerging emphatic emergent,

Enacting enormously,

End, ending endlessly,

Earning envisions Earrings

Eating early evenings

Europe, England, Egypt,

Encrypted exhausted e-mail

"Keeping existing form in mind, I have experimented and came up with two poetry forms which are Remix Poetry and Poetry Rainbow. Remix poetry is using different forms of poetry in one poem and Poetry rainbow is like "Unity in diversity". In poetry Rainbow, you have to choose seven different forms of poetry and each like of poetry consists of one poetic form", I said.

"What?". He didn't understand.

"Let me give you examples of both", I said and open the relevant pages of my notebook.

Ready

(Remix Poetry)

(Senryu + Lyrette + Acrostic+ Quatrain + Fibonacci + enclosed rhyme + Tanka)

Destruction alone

There's a Poet in Everyone

A new birth of sanity

The lord of humans

Oh Lord!

My pure soul,

Is now ready,

For humanity,

To fight evil,

To protect,

To rise

Rigorous bloody sensations,

Eating away thy soul,

Ardent believe is boiling,

Deadly sighs needs to end,

Yes, I want war,

A war for new beginning of life,

Ending all the tormented tears,

Ending that ultimate strife,

To eradicate all fears,

I,

Want,

To kill,

Pain and mask,

Dr. Diwakar Pokhriyal

And insanity

To create a world within peace

Oh lord! Give me power,

To clear off this mist of sham,

To clear off this spam,

Oh lord! Drown me in shower,

My believe in truth is intact,

I am aware of my awareness,

Ready to end the darkness,

I am standing to make this pact,

I am screaming loud,

"Come on demon let us fight",

For ultimate prize,

For holy world and the truth,

I am ready to die.

Keep writing
(Poetry Rainbow)

Never leave the thoughts alone, (free verse)

That is so bad, (Cinquian)

Know the truth, (Etheree)

Continuity rules here, (Tanka)

Waving the flag so high, (Acrostic)

There's a Poet in Everyone

Instigating inspiration, (Alleteration)
Connecting with that almighty through verses and thoughts. (Fibonacci)

"Oh, that means in rainbow form only one line follows that poetry form rule, but in remix poetry it is the complete forms combined together for one theme?", my friend said.
"Yes, you are absolutely right", I smiled.
"Heptaoem is like Heptane + poem, meaning you will have to use seven words, creating a poem and each word comes in one line. The last word would be the title of the poem", I Said.
"This is the short and crisp form", my friend applauded.
"Yes, very compact", I said and he wrote a poem.

Writing
(Heptaoem)
Misunderstood,
By,
Maximum,
Brains,
Yet,
Surviving,
Writing.

"Spot on you are", I patted his back and he laughed.
"Thank you Mr. Poet", he laughed.

"Don't you think there are lots of restrictions on the poetic forms and at times the learners lose their interest because of this", I threw a question.

"Yes, I second you", he agreed.

"So, this Freedoetry is another form that I have created. The title the mix of freedom and poetry. In this form of poetry, you can choose the number of lines in each stanza and number of stanzas, the product of two will give you number of syllables in each paragraph. Other than this there are no rules", I said.

"Oh, so it means a bit of freedom. If I choose 6 lines and 4 stanzas, then the total syllable count will be 24 in each stanza", he counted and wrote one poem.

Meaning of "Learn"
(The Freedoetry)
6 lines * 4 paragraphs = 24 syllables in each para
Learning hard,
Forgetting identity,
People in my,
Locality,
Calls it,
Necessary,

Yes it is true,
To learn things,
While forgetting,

There's a Poet in Everyone

It is absolutely true,
To even,
Learn till death,

But if,
That learning,
Does not bring satisfaction,
Does not leads me,
To light,
Not in sync with passion,

Will that be of?
Any use to,
Thy soul,
Will that ever cherish my efforts?
And construct,
My goal.

"This is amazing, you are a genius brother", he was spellbound.
"Thank you brother", I was feeling happy.
"Zig-zag rhyming poetry is another form that I experiment. In this the rhyme goes in zig zag order", I said and wrote one poem.

Around the world
(Zig-Zag rhyme)

Raise your awareness,

Dr. Diwakar Pokhriyal

Harness the hope and chase,
Base is to be built to impress,
Cess is high for the trace,

Know the world around,
Sound of air and snow,
Low and lost or found,
Bound self, you won't grow,

Prime in the perspective of you,
Clue? Go around with rhyme,
Crime shouldn't stop the dew,
New, will be your world with time.

"The last form that I tried is an encryptive poetry. All of us has heard about the encryption. I thought we can also use that in our poem", I was anxious.
"Encryption?". He was a bit shocked.
"Yes for learning, we are doing it partially, but we should increase its scale. Here is an example", I wanted to see my friend's reaction.

Encryptive Poetry - 1
Petal in Jan, Matter in Van, Ban the Love, National plan
Lion capital of Ashoka clan, Ganga rows, dolphin ran.

There's a Poet in Everyone

The Hidden Message 'National Bird, Animal, Anthem, Song, Fruit, Flower, Tree, Emblem, river and aquatic animal of INDIA'

Line - 1

PE - National Bird – Peacock

T - National Animal – Tiger

JAN - National Anthem - Jan Gan

MA - National Fruit – Mango

VA - National song – Vande Maatram,

BA - Nation Tree – Banyan

LO - National Flower – Lotus

Line -2

Lion Capital of Ashoka - National Emblem - Lion Capital of Ashoka at Sarnath

Ganga - National River – Ganga

Dolphin - National Aquatic Animal - Dolphin.

"Wow brother! This is just out of this world. These forms will inspire the aspiring write to do something new that might help us in creating our own history", his eyes were twinkling.

"Yes, this is what I want, I want everyone to enjoy poetry and be open for the experimentation. First, read different forms of poetry, understand them, practice them and then create your own legacy. Everyone is free to like any poetic form, but a poem should also add something from his or her side to the poetic world that should inspire the new blood", I said and my friend agreed.

We had a great time with each other. In last seven to eight months we had shared close to 50 forms of poetry and both of us indeed started loving poetry to the core. I never had an idea that my journey of learning poetry may come to this beautiful place, where I will start a living poetry. Indeed, there is a long road to even touch the poetry greats, but I have now started enjoying poetry and that is most important for any artist or human being. I thought about a possible future where all inspiring writers will start enjoying poetry and start painting into their canvas a new poetry form.

Chapter – 2
ABC Poem

Young Enthusiasm

A Baked Cake,

Delicious enough,

For Generating Haste,

Instigate Jerks Knowingly,

Leaving Man Nasty,

Outside Placid Quantum,

Reinforce Subtle Treasury,

Unknown Venom Wears,

Xeric Youthful Zest

Foolishness

All Baked Cookies,

Dried Elegantly,

Fists Gluing Heroically,

I Jumped Knowingly, Lethargically,

Murdered Nastily Own Pride,

Questioned Repeatedly Self,

To Understand Very Well,

X-ray Yelling Zone.

Dr. Diwakar Pokhriyal

Smiling heart

Are you so independent, that?

Blinders of mind can't flaunt you,

Colonial cousins of disaster may create upheaval,

Death will never become defunct,

Still possess that smiling heart.

Leader

Energizing lives to cross the roads,

Flawlessly flaunting the dedication,

Generating smiles for humanity,

Humanity needs to be awaken,

Thy God will lead.

Essence of humanity

Rhetoric redundancy of calamities,

Sweeps away thy solace,

Traumatizing the advent,

Umpteen losses Kills the race,

That's the essence of Humanity

Hope

A Bribed Calamity,

Designs Enough Failures,

Growing Hatred Inspires,

Just Knocks Lone Madness,

There's a Poet in Everyone

Nasty Owen Pricks Quickly,

Rest Shows Timeless, Unending, Venomous Work,

Xenophobia Yawns Zest.

Chapter – 3
Acrostic Poetry

Let The New Year Shine

Let the New Year Shine,
Engulfing all negativities,
Triumping over redundancies,

Thoughts of yesterday,
Harmonising with the future,
Emphatic present should rise,

Nostalgic moments,
Energetic actions,
Wow, let the time fly,

Yes, let's share positivity,
Enriching the youth,
Artistic seconds should tickle,
Rightfully eradicating the demonic nights,

Spread around the world,
Humbleness and harmony,
Inclusive nature of humanity,
New year should unite,
Energies, bodies, and souls.

There's a Poet in Everyone

Poetry

Poignant creatures are rare,

Omnipotent are even rarer,

Essence of humanity decreasing,

Try to elevate earth,

Reconstructing beliefs in positivity,

Yes, the language might be "Poetry"

Missing your touch

Magical moments rejuvenate,

Instigating your presence,

Sophisticated problems deceives,

Showering love in your absence,

Innate touch arise from nowhere,

Nostalgic and Never-ending

Graciously cloning your care.

Yet, my eyes shot your image,

Outrageous into blind sky,

Unrevealing my lovely angel,

Resting our love on thy.

Transforming a feeble belief,

Onto the earth of misunderstanding,

Understanding your flawless relief,

Charismatic and shiny,

Hearty and perfectly outstanding.

Chapter – 4
Abecedarian Poetry

Depression

Alas! I have lost,

Brutally, from thyself,

Ceasing to exist, now,

Duped determination

Erratic behaviour,

False belief,

Grinding thy soul,

Have faith, Oh Man!,

In the Almighty,

Just at the corner,

Kind heart and soul exists,

Lust can't win,

Moans are momentary,

Nasty clouds will fade away,

Oh, I can listen to you,

Purging my dejection,

Quitting my tale,

Rising pain, no purpose,

Slowly and steadily,

Time is ticking away,

Unity isn't an option,

Venom has acted fast,

There's a Poet in Everyone

Wishes are out of the box,

Xeroxing my erroneous fate,

Yes, I am about to sleep,

Zooming into the depressive valley.

Heart

Almost on the verge of,

Breaking the rules,

Carefree heart,

Dodged the vocal bullets, but,

Empowered tragedies,

Fierce rivalry,

Grinds him into emotions,

He happily left the battle,

In search of solace,

Jockeying around,

Keen to touch,

Letting the peace of mind, shape,

Myriad reflection of truth,

No, the heart tried and lost,

Oh! Poor heart,

Post the setback,

Questions the existence,

Rapidly disintegrating,

Solace and peace,

Total darkness,

Dr. Diwakar Pokhriyal

Untidy thoughts,

Vivacious demons,

Wetted the walls of the heart,

Xeroxing the emotional turmoil,

Yeah, the heart always loses,

Zest keeps him alive.

Chapter – 5
Alliterative Poetry

Hope and woe

Dating depression drastically,

Hope hypnotizes humans,

Warriors were born,

In the midst of thousand Trojans,

The symphonic scars of subtlety,

Sang the slice of satire,

And the annoyed angst,

Articulately arrested the attire,

Hope hanged till harmony,

Hassle free holiday awaits,

Human needs to nail the net,

To blossom those million fates,

Yes, he yorked the young,

Hope shall be wandering wishfully,

Woe will write her wrath,

 Wasting his words, gleefully

Dr. Diwakar Pokhriyal

Picture of peace

Tried and tested,

The tricks of taking the tiger home,

Brainwash the beast by birth,

Let him imagine he's a fool,

A frenetic, false and foul fist,

Is only required, race rips apart,

Heart has his homage,

But, brain basks of battle,

We all are tigers,

Brainwashed, blinded & battered,

Realization rests in peace,

We work like robots,

Too lazy, lethargic and limped,

Humanity harnessing hatred,

We need to wake up soon,

To paint a perfect picture of peace.

Chapter – 6
Aquarian Poetry

Amazed

Oh Lord!

I am amazed,

Looking at the blindness,

Of heart.

Blind me

Lost self,

During the search,

Of pleasures and treasures,

Blind me.

Write

Keep up,

The good spirit,

And write every season,

To live.

Hold

Just hold,

My arm tighter,

And let me imagine,

The love.

Wake up

Wake up,

And sleep again,

Repeat the damn process,

Robot

Pray

Sit down,

And pray for life,

Purple patch is missing,

No choice.

Chapter – 7
Baccresieze Poetry

Her sacrifice

She lived her life, only for love
She hugged the strife, only for love,
Like a prince, he was raised by her,
Her sacrifice

Imagination was all nice,
But reality knocked one day,
She lived her life, only for love
Her sacrifice

The lousy face of prince emerged,
Abandoning purity, bliss,
The time cried, humanity died,
Her sacrifice

Reality

Endless love here, is just a myth
The superman, is just a myth,
Churned between, dreams and the demon,
Reality

Feeling proud of being guilty,

Dr. Diwakar Pokhriyal

Sanity has lost the battle,
Endless love here, is just a myth
Reality

The haziness is being sold,
The packet of sensations lives,
Expectations kill the human,
Reality.

Chapter – 8
Cadence Poetry

Eureka

Great,

Brilliant,

Eureka,

An idea

Pure energy,

To drastically change the course

Of known history

Help

Help,

Those poor,

Lost creature,

Identities,

Mislead bodies

For regaining their confidence,

To conquer their fear

Passion

True,

Passion,

And true hope,

Is destiny

Of a warrior,

That paints entire burning canvas,

With his fortitude.

Remember

Love,

And hate,

Are best friends,

Unknowingly

Or knowingly,

We all blindly discriminate,

To create chaos

Misread

Words

Often

We misread,

As momentum,

Inertia,

Needs much deeper understanding,

Than just being words

Competition

Waste,

Of time,

So clearly,

There's a Poet in Everyone

Competition,

Repetitions,

A tragic trap for all humans,

To live without life.

Chapter – 9
Cinquian Butterfly Poetry

Power

Power,

Is absolute,

It converts a human,

Either into a bloody beast,

Hungry,

Or into resilient saint,

What is your destiny?

That can be seen,

Clearly.

Teach

Teach me,

Oh wise teacher,

About that divine truth

And shameful agony of false,

So that,

I can calculate my worst pain,

Of facing the true false

Or the false truth

Of life.

There's a Poet in Everyone

Darkness

I was,

Oh my dear lord,

Totally Afraid of,

That darkness resting inside me

As I,

Scared identity of human,

Knows that horrible truth

Of dark failure,

And death

Your voice

Your voice,

Is beautiful,

Oh my divine partner,

It sounds perfect as melody

To me,

And my ever innocent heart,

Like a crazy lover

Melts instantly,

With smile

Books

Great friends,

For the life time,

Teaching our inner self,

Dr. Diwakar Pokhriyal

True humanity and pure love,

Touching,

All our careless lives forever

As Shining sun of hope

Create inside,

Heaven.

Chapter – 10
Cinquian

Faith

Trust me,

When I hug tight,

And kiss you in the rain,

The moments dissolve into me,

Like you.

Magic

Look at,

The magical,

Also the tragical,

Game of life, that turns us into,

Puppet

Door

Close it,

And introspect,

The opening required,

To rise from the ashes, to write,

The fame.

Chapter – 11
Couplets

There is a place where the sidewalks end,
Happiness prevails, forgetting the trend,

The scent of the soul, energizes the man,
Leaving for the humanity, a hidden clan,

And the twinkling starts glorifies the way,
Shooting every moment, Want's to say,

'Oh Human, repercussion of blind love,
Creates the jail, an antonym of the dove,

The flow stops at the place of meditation,
Heart dwells the positivity and the elation,

The rainbow of attires diminishes at will,
The murmurs of the angels that sat still,

Tiny desires and mammoth fires inside,
Chemical reactions that dissolve pride,

Yes, there is a place where awaits a friend,
Yes, there is a place where the sidewalks end…

Memories
(9 Couplets)

Catastrophe isn't incessant raining blood,
It's that piece of land, where we last stood,

Where I lost the charm of my flickering life,
Every twinkling second turned into a strife,

Where all the fairies lost to an ugly reality,
Loneliness was my gift, painted brutality,

Where fragrance seized to exist any more,
A black box in this puny earth with no door,

Where tragedy stuns the humanity and smile,
Pervert time keeps you alive, death is style,

Where plethora of event pleads to respond,
And the silence of soul breaks every bond,

Where words lose the battle to numbness,
And a body is only left, nothing to harness,

Where a tide sweeps the heart at the shore,
The bed of tempting roses, no more a galore

Dr. Diwakar Pokhriyal

The touch of love, leaves you at intersections,
And when you believe in it, only rejections…

Chapter – 12
Cromorna

Lesson

Spring in the summer,

With fire,

A quest for glimmer,

With desire,

Life is vehicle,

You, tyre,

For Happy cycle,

A buyer,

They will only share,

An attire,

And who am I here?

A liar.

Thoughts

A hope with the god,

Is a lie,

You think I am fraud?

Go and fly,

Our time is finite,

We will die,

Oh this starry night,

A decoy,

You always treat me,

As a toy,

And still you believe,

In full pie?

Chapter – 13
Diagonal Acrostic

Weight

Waiting till ages,

The enormous hope of life,

Trying to integrate the wellness,

Understanding the real gist of the talk,

All of it, in hope of getting,

Weight behind my words and try.

Time

Test your skills,

And initiate,

The holy masculine love,

For catering, feminine ego.

Right

Rough estimates,

Just indicates the desperation,

Engulfing the great fear,

That can be heightened instantly,

Painting the wrong as right.

Dr. Diwakar Pokhriyal

Chapter – 14
Double Acrostic

Know your strength

Kindness needs to come back

Nasty truth breaks the plan,

Outplayed humanity too,

Woes overburdening smiles now,

Yell off the decoy,

Omnipresent god is in zoo,

Uttering flawless you,

Rise and fall is your décor,

Stand for your believes,

Timeless faith in rest,

Rowdiness shouldn't soar,

Enigma of death isn't nice,

Never ending hope is the plan

Go for peace and a smiling bag,

Tiredness is virtue of defeat,

Heinous acts shouldn't rest a sigh.

Dance

Dance away the retard,

Arrogance isn't faithful saga,

There's a Poet in Everyone

Naughtiness of heart is clan,

Clean and powerful as Mac,

Emerging as perfect friend of glee.

Ready to Fight

Repercussions of a war,

Enters deep inside,

Altitude filled era,

Dried and yet glad,

Yes I am talking about joy,

Tasty food also takes rust,

Omnipresent is yet a big no,

Fight is only a decision half,

Inspiring millions to believe in 'I',

Gruesome mentality of fog,

Heights of deadly wrath,

Totally blind leaves humanity aghast.

Close to you

Crimson color of your havoc,

Lightness of kisses depicting zeal,

Overwhelming touch of you too,

Seizing my golden moments of bliss,

Energies rebuilding inside me,

Dr. Diwakar Pokhriyal

Timeless scent of your waist,
Out bursting emotions to do,

Your presence makes me a coy,
Omnipresent is your smile, ready to go,
Unaltered sky of adore is my love only you.

War of Blinds
Worried eyes are bleeding now,
Astonished hearts singing the raga,
Rowdiness is becoming now a war,

Outnumbered believers of sanity too,
Fractured brains are completely off,

Blinds of today needs no stab,
Lethargy in actions and the deal,
Indecisiveness of humans and their "Hi",
Normality and abnormality of their plan,
Death isn't their goal so sad,
Slender sign of happiness is their carcass.

Chapter – 15
Duodara

Never Pretend

Never Pretend,

To be correct or wrong,

Life is a full circle

Swinging pendulum

An unknown darkness,

And also an enlightening journey,

Who knows at which quadrant you will die,

Never Pretend,

To go into the books

Of trust and friendship,

Of pure emotions,

Of goodness and hope

Without having a wholesome human heart,

Because if you are then it is a lie.

Musically

Musically,

Your every second rocks,

And energy flows,

Within your chaste soul

Gifting you those dreams

That converts hope to reality here,

And ignites a spark of better human,

Musically,

You connect to yourself,

In much deeper sense,

Earth, sky and fire,

Water and ether,

You find within with positivity,

Very thin line between god and demon.

Rhythm

Rhythm of life

Is very important,

Gives us energy,

New thoughts and new ways,

Refreshes our mind,

Keeps us away from unwanted evil,

Keeps us away from negativity.

Rhythm of life,

A creator so true,

Of our character,

Of our destiny,

Of our decisions,

Prepare us for stringent and dark battles,

And gift us hope and positivity.

Chapter – 16
Echo Verse

End

Control your uncanny surge,

Urge,

Good and bad can't merge,

Urge,

Oh Boy, fanatically you have to diverge,

Urge

Consider it as reality or as hormonal,

Zonal,

Now weeds cannot converge

Urge,

Stop praying for profound spring

Ring

Even saints are now fanatical and selfish,

Fish

No time for you to pretend

End

Misbehavior you should only Attend

End

Nothing in this lifeless world you can amend

End

Forget to paint a phoenix or a trend

End

All the wall are broken you can't mend,

End

Your hands are fiercely broken you can't lend

End

Iterations of desires knows no bend

End

Oh my noxious human you have reached the dead end

End

Stable

What will make your life stable,

Able,

Oh! The desire to win winks,

Inks,

And what remains with humanity,

Tea,

What people freely share?

Air,

Yes and that's so true,

You,

But stability is far away,

Way,

Yes, there is a way for sure,

Your,

Rest in peace and rusticate,

Gate.

Chapter – 17
Enclosed Rhyme

Sleepy

The eyes have lost the battle,
The body hangs in the air,
Oh lord, it's not fair,
I'm wandering like a cattle,

This work of mine,
Is killing me more,
Can't see the door,
I think I'm not fine,

The time is adamant,
Running away from me,
Yet to identify the spree,
My worries are permanent,

Give me extra time,
To complete my life,
I am fed up of this strife,
So, I completed this rhyme.

Dr. Diwakar Pokhriyal

Relationship

So swift and so sweet,
Your smile has magic,
My life is so tragic,
As if two ends can't meet,

Yet, I will give a try,
To rip apart the pain,
To train the lane,
To paint the sky,

Yes, I know this for sure,
Tragedy will block my way,
Carcasses will haunt, have their say,
But passion will find a cure,

And we will become one soul,
Dissolving into each other eyes,
Living together the sighs,
We will converge our goal.

Chapter – 18
Epitaphs

Epitaph-1

Where were you when I was alive?

Where were you when I was counting five,

Don't waste your time here,

You better leave and live your strife.

Epitaph-2

I realize this,

People will not let you live,

And when you are dead,

Will not let you sleep

Epitaph-3

I have enough time now,

Do you know why?

I fell in love instantly,

Without inspecting that guy.

Epitaph-4

Now who will ruin your life,

Who will make you tremble,

Oh! A poet is now dead,

Who will write your fumble?

Epitaph-5

Give me money in my grave,

Come to me if you are brave,

I challenge you to play with grace,

If you win, You can take my place.

Chapter – 19
Etheree

Masked Freedom

High,

On beer,

Feeling proud,

And ecstatic,

Forgetting the truth,

Forgetting existence

Forgetting self, is one way,

To prepare self to run away

To prepare self for devastation,

Masked as enjoyment and freedom in life.

Table

Have,

You seen,

Besides you,

That lone table,

That keeps the things, high,

Giving a lot of space,

Never let them fall off them

Can we human, become like them

Lifting people up, holding them up,

Inspire them to achieve their ambitions.

Dr. Diwakar Pokhriyal

Chapter – 20
Double Etheree

Realization,

I,

Woke up,

To find out,

Hidden treasure,

In the shining sun

In the dancing droplets,

In the shades of lovely trees,

In the chills of flowing wind,

In the chirping of freedom around,

When suddenly I heard a voice, Alas!

Realization of crude emotions,

Realization of emptiness,

Realization of the pain,

Realization of hate,

Realization of,

Realization,

I slept again,

In hope of,

A new,

Life.

There's a Poet in Everyone

Open the Door

Rest,

At peace,

With the life,

By opening,

All the doors you see,

The door of acceptance,

The door of pure elation,

The door of that togetherness,

The door of hope and positive vibes,

The door of determination and love

And shut the doors down with all precision,

The door of comparison and hate,

The door of religious blindness,

The door of all temptations,

The door of disbelief,

The door of black greed,

The door of crimes,

The door of,

Thoughts that,

Kills.

Dr. Diwakar Pokhriyal

Chapter – 21
Etheree Reverse

War of Aggression

Sparkling eyes were hypnotized to kill truth,

To rule the empire of dissonance,

To craft an era of freedom,

I crawled into aggression,

In the end of the war,

I lost my desires,

And my passion,

And my Hope,

My life,

Me.

Determined to rise

I know my path will be filled with dangers,

Timeless harassments and touching tears,

Broken hopes and those shattered dreams,

Demon will be empowered,

But I will keep running,

I will be the one,

A perfect soul,

Determined,

To rise,

High.

There's a Poet in Everyone

United in love

Sudden temptation of beauty and bliss

Is history and gone forever

For never ending sensations

Now your touch is just enough,

Only need to close eyes

To grasp your presence,

And to feel as,

United,

You and,

Me.

Dr. Diwakar Pokhriyal

Chapter – 22
Etheree Twin Double

Unity

We,

See,

Just I,

Lone thy,

Loses fun,

Love gets stun,

Unity just rocks,

Fixes all blocks

Teamwork always glow,

No matter how slow,

Aloofness kills slowly

Company is holy

Let's unite to fill the gap,

A shower under same tap,

We are just born to love and care,

There's a Poet in Everyone
Playing jointly with equal share

Under the sky of serenity,
Inside deep blue sea of dignity

A layer of firm trust lies there anew,
Understood by true souls which are left few,

A time to spread this important message,
Driving this sleeping and empty carriage,

It's time, wake up for agility,
Now silently kill humility

The beautiful flower of hope,
With fragrance of truth without dope

Swimming in sea of passion,
Without fear of recession

Flirting with naughty fate,
As if opening gate,

Gate of real trust,
Where love enter "must"

Dr. Diwakar Pokhriyal

Finding true friends

Changing old trends

Purity,

Unity,

Sees right,

No fight,

We,

Flee.

Choice

Try,

High,

The call,

The wall,

Rise today,

Have your say,

World is rising,

Know the pricing,

Scintillating time,

There's a Poet in Everyone
Creates perfect rhyme,

Collect all the moments,
Keep checking your movements,

Life is so full of challenges,
Never boils for revenges,

Paint the sun and pick up the stars,
Count the blessings and not the scars,

The spring and youth can turn it around,
Scrambled humanity knows no bound,

The will and determination shall shine,
Like the leaves of autumn and like a wine,

But, if you shall choose the dark path of wrong,
Oh, poor human, you will mess up the song,

And the night of pain shall come haunting
All tasks in life, would turn as daunting,

Volcano eruption will stay,
Your moments will end at the bay,

Dr. Diwakar Pokhriyal

There will only be the pain,
No happiness and no gain,

The world will become bleak,
No glimpse of shining peak,

Brain will kill the heart,
No jewels, just dirt,

So, be aware,
And take full care,

Bend the fears,
And shift gears,

Learn rights,
Reach heights,

Prize,
Rise.

Chapter – 23
Etheree Twin

My love

Sweet,

Greet,

Leaves me,

In glee,

Lovely wish,

Or nice dish,

A smile of you,

Leaves without clue,

Like the wind so swift,

As a precious gift,

Like a touch of fingers,

Where only love lingers,

You are here so merciful,

An angel so beautiful,

A touchy shower for my soul

Dr. Diwakar Pokhriyal

You are only romantic goal,

Instigating care and trust inside,
For taking an everlasting stride,

Resting inside continuous hear beat,
You are "My Love", so cute, bubbly and sweet.

Decision

Lies,

Sighs,

Connects,

Rejects,

Bathe so bright,

Absent light,

Wounds so badly,

Searching madly,

A body and soul,

Like a cocky goal,

To instill fear inside,

With hollow and weak pride,

There's a Poet in Everyone
To make humanity weak
Painting our future so bleak,

Negativity walks besides,
Where positivity resides,

Choose very wisely for that instance,
Don't live a life soaked in repentance,

As you all are special powers of lord,
Always pluck that most melodious chord.

Music
Hear,
Clear,

That note,
Lone boat,

Parody,
Melody,

That soothes your mind,
That makes you blind,

Take you to heaven,

Dr. Diwakar Pokhriyal
All above seven,

Makes you to fly so high,
As if you own whole sky,

Leaves you in full ecstasy
Changes your reality,

Let you feel the essence of life,
Erasing the presence of strife,

That is power of music so pure,
Like a natural and herbal cure,

It makes you forget anything tragic,
Touches your soul to create magic.

Chapter – 24
English Ghazal

Afterlife

I experienced life, in the midst of chaos
I have trusted a knife, in the midst of chaos

I can not pick up the stars, walking on this earth,
So I entrusted the strife, in the midst of chaos,

Lost inside the blankness of colorful desires,
I Looked solace as wife, in the midst of chaos,

Such emotional tremors hit me so often,
This silent night looks rife, in the midst of chaos,

Walking with melancholy thought 'Oh My Dear friend'
Thinking what's afterlife, in the midst of chaos.

A long time

I have felt the rain, after a long time,
I have felt the pain, after a long time,

Memories are just endless and cruel,
I boarded that train, after a long time,

Dr. Diwakar Pokhriyal

Step by step, I have reached the twinkling stars,
Forgetting my lane, after a long time,

Planning isn't my cup of tea, I think,
God needs me to train, after a long time,

Time is the best healer 'O My Friend',
Understood refrain, after a long time.

Chapter – 25
Fibonacci

Zest

Have,

Zest,

To rise,

Against odds,

To pounce and bounce, to,

Cement emphatic legacy,

Which is born out of sheer determination to win.

Cry

Cry,

Now,

Letting,

Your soul free,

Of all the past sins,

To write a page in history,

And to revive the fallen humanity, to live.

Faith

Have,

Faith,

Oh Man!

In yourself,

But, be determined,

Most importantly, to succeed,

And keep honing your skills to cement your faith in faith.

Chapter – 26
Free Verse

Fun

Am I in the clouds?

The child danced feeling sound,

No son, it's winter,

A lot to play around,

We ran endlessly,

Stop, I am tired,

I looked right and left,

And shook my head,

Do you know which road we traced?

You are new here? He danced,

He danced and rejoiced,

I love the road which leads to nowhere,

Oh, I can listen to myself,

How come here? He was puzzled,

You should have studied son,

Mountains are right here,

Oh, but what about them,

He signaled towards few bodies,

Those who were free from physical square,

Speechless, I said, the stars are their attire.

Tragedy

He hid from me long ago,
I am still unable to find,
Oh Lord! Give me hope,
The tragedy stabbed me,
Ripped my soul apart,
I am still breathing death,
Second by second,
That sunny day of curse,
And night of black magic,
Spine chilling moments,
Unforgettable tears,
Insane atmosphere,
I was just few steps away,
When my sea of emotions,
Drowned in the sea of water,
And like a numb,
I lived my life as death.

Chapter – 27
Glosa

Glosa- 1

First four Lines taken from Sarojini Naidu's poem - 'Autumn Song'

Like a joy on the heart of a sorrow,
The sunset hangs on a cloud;
A golden storm of glittering sheaves,
Of fair and frail and fluttering leaves,

Temptations and reality of the life,
Unmatched and untouched,
Misunderstood sanity, blind faith,
Humanity has lost the touch,
Roads are full, but hearts are empty,
Tears are waived off of emotion,
Only money and money rules,
No shoulder to cry on,
But we want to see the moon in elation,
Like a joy on the heart of a sorrow,

The leaves fall off with a smile,
Oh! You forgot my love,
The timeless demon that kills,
The timeless sighs that tears apart,

Dr. Diwakar Pokhriyal

And in the pain that is eternal,

The smile is just a mask,

A mask that makes you happy,

For an instant and then leaves,

Like a night, and to complete a task,

The sunset hangs on a cloud;

Yet, I know this loneliness,

Can still bring me the strength,

The positivity to survive,

In this world of black magic,

In this world of tragedies,

In this world of satire,

A ray of hope climbs,

The mountain of blemishes,

Like a tornado of burning fire,

A golden storm of glittering sheaves,

So, it's time to rethink,

And dive into the silent valley,

The pearl is somewhere inside,

It's time we should understand,

The filth we are painting,

It's time we should disperse,

To re-unite at the dawn,

And I love this thought,

There's a Poet in Everyone

And I love this pretty universe,
Of fair and frail and fluttering leaves,

Glosa- 2

The first four lines are of the poem 'My Garden Smiles' by Dr APJ Abdul Kalam.

My garden smiles
Welcoming the spring,
Roses, beautiful roses,
With fragrance and beauty,

My country gives me hope,
To share the love,
The history is rich,
The present has potential,
Changing paradigms,
I feel the power of youth,
The bright stars of tomorrow,
Possessing the zeal,
Looking at the power of truth,
My garden smiles

It smiles for the hope,
For the scenic beauty,
For the unity of us,
That takes us through,

Dr. Diwakar Pokhriyal

In the times of struggle,

And I know that we will,

Cross the barriers of words,

That pulls us down,

But, we will keep alive the thrill,

Welcoming the spring,

And then there would be happiness,

None would be careless,

There would be hugs,

There would be pride,

There would be a help,

No differences, only the sum,

The angel would be here,

Amused at the purity,

And then we will become,

Roses, beautiful roses,

And the world will shine,

With the reign of glory,

Oh! What a beautiful thought,

The youth will bring the change,

With determination and creativity

The youth will live in that time,

Oh! I can see the sprouting hope,

The universe will then shrink,

There's a Poet in Everyone

The life will become a poem with rhyme,
With fragrance and beauty.

Chapter – 28
Golda Poetry

Waiting

A glimpse,

Of you,

Keeps me alive,

In,

This rotten world

Oh love,

The sighs,

Weeps,

Often,

Fearing of death,

When we fly high,

Like dove.

Mist

The mist,

Around,

Never stops you,

From,

Touching your dreams

Alive,

What stops,

Us,

Indeed,

Is disbelief,

Towards peace and,

The life.

Abandoned

Was Shocked,

By life,

Sky cried aloud,

Oh!

And the earth drowned,

In shame,

Alas!

He,

Left her,

In old age home,

Just to search for,

The fame.

Chapter – 29
Haiku & Senryu

Vibes

Steal the silent spring,

And sprinkle water around,

The positive vibes

Childhood

Spring of stars around,

Childhood reminiscences,

The night becomes day.

Dream

Spring of sensations,

Painting the life's ecstasy,

A dream of a dream

Wish

Your Tranquility,

Oxygen of my terrain,

A wishful thinking.

Chapter – 30
Lai Poetry

Just see

Do trust your own feel,

Do check your own deal,

Trust me,

Wins you have to seal,

Perfection is reel,

Just me,

Only thing to steal

In a day, a meal,

Just see.

Write it

If there is a pain,

If there is a rain,

Write it,

If you lost the lane,

If you missed the train

Find it

If you want to train,

Or craft a terrain

Fight it.

Dr. Diwakar Pokhriyal

Chapter – 31
The Lyrette

Sense

Nonsense,

Is this world,

That fights for truth,

Misunderstanding,

Meaning of peace,

Pays the price,

With life

Humiliation

Flowers

Everywhere,

Are being crushed,

Humiliating

Humanity

Ashamed of,

Itself

Amazing

Wishful,

Amazing,

And breathtaking

Is our precious life,

There's a Poet in Everyone

Always believe,

In yourself,

Oh Man!

Friend

My friend,

Understands,

My lone silence,

My deepest regret,

Ready to craft,

Magical,

Friendship

Smile with me

Now Smile,

Forever,

Live Happily,

To create heaven,

To end demise

And to smile,

With me

Artist

Artists,

Crafting hope,

For living world,

For Humanity,

For truth and light,

Creating,

Magic.

Chapter – 32
The Marianne

Wings

I have those wings,

For the humanity,

Wings of desire, fire and swings,

Let that lone sweet,

Bell rings

Misunderstanding

Timelessness,

Black hole of sanity,

No one inculcates and harness

And no body,

Impress.

Rest

Give rest to mind,

From insane ideas,

You need time to calmly rewind,

To rise and to,

Be kind.

Dr. Diwakar Pokhriyal

Decide

Choose your fortune

And always play harder,

Why consider luck from Neptune?

Keep enjoying,

The tune

Vehicle

Mechanical,

Yet assists the human,

Is it the mindset cynical,

Or attitude,

Fickle

Loss

Cost of a loss,

Unbearable and vast,

But situations are like toss,

Profit here is,

Not gross.

Chapter – 33
Nonet

Night

The baby steps we had together,

Are now, memories of the day,

The shiny smile and the hug,

Looks distant and lost now,

Darkness prevails here,

Inside my soul,

You were the,

Only,

Hope.

Hype

Have you heard about cacophony?

That divides the human notion

That tears all people apart,

In quest of becoming,

Something you desire,

But that desire,

Is merely,

A pure,

Hype.

Chapter – 34
Quatrain

Humanity

Entwined in thoughts,

Life lives at the junction,

Everyone has empty slots

Yet, the humanity is busy in function

Grip

Do not tighten the hold,

The pigeon may die soon,

In the pursuit of the gold,

You might lose the moon.

Remember

If you want greatness,

In your depleting stocks,

You'll have to harness,

Those chilling shocks

Emphatic Life

Emphatic life is the consequence,

Of a determined soul,

Keeping alive your innocence,

Keeping alive hope for the goal.

Chapter – 35
Quintet (English)

Waiting for love

I held you hands my love,

In pursuit of freshness and care,

You flew away like a dove,

Reflecting deepest fear of share,

Never thought Oh love! How could I dare,

You are my love so pure,

Every touch of yours instill life,

You are my penultimate cure,

Above my every single strife,

But oh love, you killed my hope with a knife.

Yet love knows no barrier,

I am still breathing in your wait,

You are my only carrier,

Towards that heaven's gate,

I am waiting, please come back Oh mate!

Light

I can see that dim hope,

Shivering due heavy disbelief,

Absolute truth wants to elope,

In search of some relief,

But Alas! We termed it as a thief.

Dr. Diwakar Pokhriyal

Hope

Alas! This world is bleeding to hell,
Yet none is preparing for this war,
Magnetic currency wants to tell,
The embarrassing price of the scar,
Let's hope for the morning, let's hope for a star.

Save

Slumber epitaphs of lives are many,
Everyone is lost inside mist of believe,
Journey of true passion is uncanny,
Courageous warriors have to retrieve,
Resulting into a rain of disbelieve,

Oh Lord! That shining courageous light,
Is now really nowhere to be seen,
How could we turn a day into night,
Giving useless reasons, so umpteen,
Showcasing the almighty as mean,

It's time to reviver our power,
We need to introspect hard,
Thinking under magical shower,
We have to complete that yard,
To stop the universe from becoming retard.

Chapter – 36
Rhyming

Lantern

How can I forget,
Those moments so pure,
The world for me was blank,
Yet, I was so sure,

I walked away being sure,
Without analyzing the point,
In that brutal instant,
I broke that lovely joint,

Oh Dad! How mad was I,
Thinking of my own life,
Instantly coloring black,
Your tears and your strife,

And now at this point,
When I am alone,
Every second I hear,
Your lovely tone,

God might have taken,
Your body in a turn,

Your love & your wisdom,
Will remain my lantern.

Why O Why

Why o Why,
You are in between,
I'm not in my childhood,
I'm not it my teen,

Let me conquer the world,
Moving ahead with passion,
Come along with me,
Don't fear about recession,

Together we shall win,
Erasing every adversity,
Let us join the forces,
To challenge every calamity,

Why o Why,
You scare of failure,
Life is variable,
Fear has got no cure,

Let me dance on my tune,
I shall create a new tone,

Don't be scared of time,
If I'll not fall, how will I hone,

Why O why,
You are being the hindrance,
I want us to be together,
To craft a new entrance,

O my parents,
I am not against you,
I want to be me,
I want to be the dew.

Moments

Can you see in my eyes?
She was trying to romanticize,
Can't you see the white mirror around?
Oh, it took an hour to summarize,

Where are we? She exclaimed,
The GPS failed at her tone,
Inquiring all the possible degrees,
I rested my bums on the stone,

Oh my that mean we are…?
Yes, your indication is right,

Dr. Diwakar Pokhriyal

What would I have said,
To make her situation tight,

We ran kilometers & she screamed,
Got scared by her own voice,
Oh my, that's a phenomena,
Bad deed comes back to rejoice,

Luckily Her eyes found a child,
Shivering with cold, in tears,
Where is your home child?
He smiled and said, Nowhere!

It touched her from inside,
Forgetting her own plight,
She wrapped the child in her warmth,
And the day overcame the night.

Love

Tread lightly, she is near, Under the snow,
Look at her face, her smile and her glow,

You will transcend all the known barriers,
Falling in love, you'll find all the careers,

And then dive into the sea of sacredness,

There's a Poet in Everyone

Oh creator of agony, the love is to harness,

The timeless feeling will fill you with life,
Immersed in the sense of adore, no strife,

The fragrance of positivity and humanity,
Love will melt your heart and melt sanity,

Beware of her tears, Beware of her fears,
Love is the vehicle of life, changing gears,

Hug her tight to forget the world around,
Whisper care with love and she'll be sound

Hold her through thick, thin and otherwise,
She is you, you are her, this isn't a surprise

And fight with her endlessly for realization,
The presence is to be shown with sensation,

Kiss her, gently, until she melts in your arms,
Dissolve her into your soul, devoid of harms,

And then travel through the time and write,
The love story so sacred, stars of the night.

Dr. Diwakar Pokhriyal

Painting

Tears of blood are incessant,
They lived that, what I meant,

Sacrificing the identity for us,
And we react to them as a bus,

Unwary & unmoved they smile,
And we hide ourselves in style,

Burning terrain or freezing rain,
For these hero's, where's the pain,

It's time to wake up, Oh my Nation,
The time has come for the elation,

Carcasses are to be buried, deep,
Let's paint the happiness to keep,

We are together, we need to show,
We are on the same boat, let's row,

Fears of the poor and the rejection,
Let's rejoice in life, no dejection,

No politics of greed and no masks,

There's a Poet in Everyone

Let's live together, sharing tasks,

A small step of millions if added,
Will stun the world and stranded,

Stranded of positivity, hope, light,
Painting love, future would be bright,

Oh my dear souls, leave differences,
We need hugs, not the conferences.

Friend Forever

They say friends are forever and stay till the end,
Do they really understand, who set this trend?

Awe inspired and ecstatic, I watched you dance,
Outburst emotion and adrenaline rush at a glance,
You hugged her tight in the assurance of the sea,
Compassion at your feet and the life breaks for tea,

The rain turned into drizzles, no excitement to trace
Life is nothing more than just a superfluous race,
When you often turned into a volcano, I was there,
The reality was taking its toll and it was crystal clear,

The heart breaks and loneliness were then evident,

Dr. Diwakar Pokhriyal

Twinkling with you, I knew nothing was permanent,
But you silently fade away towards dodgy choices,
I wanted to tear them apart, but I had no voices

Then you spent more time with me without realizing,
Your life was living, the carcasses of uneven sizing,
You uttered your pain and pleasures directly to me,
And I swam into the tsunami, that all I can see,

Today, You are burning for freedom, slow and steadily,
Oh, I just forgot, with you, I'm also burning silently
The whole atmosphere is on an inert pause, around,
My existence without you, have no meaning or bound,

I watched since your first gasp, had grown with you,
Sometimes in the day, sometimes in dark and blue,
You played with me when you were a kid or out,
And I, being your Shadow, dies with you to sprout.

Chapter – 37
SESTINA Poetry

Against the Order

Look at this slip,

Let me throw this on fire,

You murky teen,

You need to train,

Your brain, life is rough,

Will you stand the test?

What the hell is this Test?

I'll never slip,

The road is not rough,

I have in me the fire,

Go catch your train,

I am the power, I am the teen,

Yes, you careless teen,

You can't pass this test,

You should catch a train,

Get lost, you will slip,

And burn in fire,

Your life will be rough,

My life would be rough?

Dr. Diwakar Pokhriyal

I am a powerful teen,
I possess within, a fire,
A fire burning, need a test?
I will stand tall after every slip,
You can't understand, go catch a train,

Ha ha ha, catch a train?
You are a loser, becoming rough,
I am sure you will slip,
You are overconfident, frail teen,
You can't even stand a chance in a test,
And you talk about the fire?

Yes, I am the fire,
I can train,
My brain will clear the test,
I will win, no matter how rough,
I am the power, I am the teen,
You can'd bring me down, you can only watch, if I'll slip.

The fire kept burning and life became rough,
The train was off track, for both adult and teen,
Who shall pass this test? Or both will slip?

On the tip

Sitting on the tip,
Today, I feel so light,
I feel so fit,
I can see the base,
Can see the target, that I can hit,
Mark my words, Mark the date,

Yes mark this date,
While sitting at the tip,
I can see, I am a hit,
I am the messenger of light,
My creativity has no base,
In this world, I'm no fit,

In every lock same key doesn't fit,
But the idea is same for every date,
No one bothers about the base,
Every one ready to give a tip,
No one will make you feel light,
Ready to pull you down, ready to hit,

To make yourself a hit,
You have to be fit,
The demons will take away the light,
While you will have a date,

Dr. Diwakar Pokhriyal

Remember this, take it as a tip,
You know your baby like the base,

I think I need a military base,
To continuously hit,
All disasters at the tip,
This violence on mine will fit,
The time and the date,
And then I'll feel so light,

I am in search of a light,
That will take me to the base,
Don't know about that date,
When that incredible idea will hit,
And everyone will be fit,
Can someone give me the tip?

Searching for light, I might hit,
Getting the base, getting fit,
I will write the date in history, when everyone will be on the tip.

Chapter – 38
Streambed Quintet

Battle

Alas! This world is now hell,

Soul wants to yell,

Prepare for the war,

Kill the scar,

Only win to smell.

Decide your destiny now,

No matter how,

Dig down deep inside,

With the pride,

Perfect time is now

Instigation

Allow me to play, Oh Lord!

Natural chord,

Of my own powers,

In showers,

Becoming land lord,

And then I will realize,

And finalize,

True path of future,

Dr. Diwakar Pokhriyal

My nature,

And will grab my prize.

Chapter – 39
Tetractys

Love

Look,

Deep down,

Into my soul,

And find your love,

Shaping my thoughts, shaping my desires.

Flow

Come,

And flow,

Into the,

Starry lone sky,

And become my eternal moon, for life.

Depth

Deep,

Inside,

You know that,

There is something,

That connects us timelessly, is this love?

Dr. Diwakar Pokhriyal

Chapter – 40
The Kerf Poetry

Find a way

Oh my! I am livid,

Where are my empty plates?

I am poor by mind not by my actions,

But flaw is the cupid,

That can turn around our fates,

Just we have to keep checking reactions,

Lacking food might turn bad,

Forcing innocents to lie,

Who will save these chaste ballast emotions?

Let us not become sad,

Let us find something to tie

To move together in worst rejections

The game of believe

Trust, failures, tears and stars,

Life is a game of belief,

Create masterpiece with authority,

Rise above deadly scars,

Simplicity is relief,

You are a part of holy trinity,

It is termed as attire,

The jewel of life and hope

Yes very true and its simplicity,

Belief is fierce fire,

An important useful dope

Use this chance with tact and audacity.

Chapter – 41
Triplets

Playground

Playground is a place to find treasure,

Umpteen skills would be present to measure,

Battling every second forgetting the leisure.

Girlfriend

Taken as an act of proud,

Making the negativity shroud,

Last screams are so clear and loud.

Trying

Hardest thing is to do now,

Is to keep trying somehow,

And then to think on the main "How".

Star

Twinkling continuously so stark,

Creating inside us that spark,

Inspiring all of us to leave a mark.

There's a Poet in Everyone

Notes

Dancing body and dancing goal,

Music is something that touch the soul,

Always play in our life an important role.

My love

Raining flowers in your words so sweet,

Writing your name in every tweet,

Our love story will always be so neat.

Maths

I tried to locate the numbers,

Tried with few plumbers,

It ended in cutting the cucumbers.

Science

The gravity of love is more,

Scientific batsmen cannot score,

This subject should be out of store.

Football

Strategies are made and broken,

Every manger has his token,

Leaving the spectators frozen.

Dr. Diwakar Pokhriyal

The battle ground

Designed to create the heroes,

Designed to abate the zeroes,

The battle ground is a place for heroes.

Mother

Unmatched love and care,

Perfect person to talk and share,

Synonym of God and always fair.

Black

A colour considered as bleak,

Like a person named as weak,

It is our misconception at its peak.

Race

There is no end of this race,

Needless, baseless leaving no trace,

Life is to love and embrace.

Pain

Unbearable and cruel feeling,

An unwanted and dreadful dealing,

Pain is always hyped more than healing.

There's a Poet in Everyone

Tears

Countless tears were raining,

Every beat of my heart was paining,

"Why you left me alone", this thought is continuously training.

Lost

Unable to track my presence,

Seems everything is right with my absence,

Then why am I so tense?

Target

Frozen eyes and frozen mind,

Senses at its best to grind,

Just a lone stretch when you will find.

Holding hands

The biggest bliss is not the bands,

It's not even standing over all brands,

It is just sitting quietly with your love, holding hands.

Dancing

Dancing continuously forgetting time,

Repeating the words and the rhyme,

Enjoying endlessly, eradicating those moments which were lime.

Dr. Diwakar Pokhriyal

Chapter – 42
Tricubes Poetry

Lost Way

I have read,

Till my death,

All known books,

But never,

Ever tried

To read self,

And so lost,

My own way,

When alive

Silence

Understand,

The meaning,

Of silence,

Otherwise,

There will be,

No meaning,

Of the words,

That you speak,

To others

Chapter – 43
Treochair Poetry

Tell a tale

Tell a tale,

To the minds and to the hearts

They can stand or swiftly sail

Let them see,

Beyond the normal eyes,

Experience the silent sea,

Male, Female,

They are all equivalent

To embrace them, tell a tale

There's a Poet in Everyone

Life is what?

Life is what?

An empty glass of water,

Or just a shining door, shut,

Or is it,

Lost battle before the end,

A Skeptical silent pit

No one knows,

Yet, they preach about the same

To paint for the world, new lows.

Dr. Diwakar Pokhriyal

Chapter – 44
Tanka

Perspective

Just out of the blue,

A Scintillating glory

Or tragedy rule,

Life is biased, is unfair,

Meaningful or a decoy

Smile

Contagious weapon,

Use it, or, just abuse it

Confused Human brain,

It solves infinite problems,

Or it kills you instantly

Eyes

Insane battleground,

Killing millions wishfully,

The phoenix still rise,

For his ultimate demise,

Killed by the sighs and the eyes.

There's a Poet in Everyone

Rain

Wetting my body

In the search of purity,

Insane ambition,

Clouds, wondering at my feet,

Rain of sweat is bearing fruits.

Chapter – 45
A Tritina

Decision to play

In a sweet, touching day,
I was out to play,
Oh Gosh! I lost my way,

This is not the way,
I was supposed to open the day,
With a fantabulous play,

But Alas! No trace of my play,
I couldn't find my way,
What an unfortunate day,

But I will change this day when I will play after finding my way.

Write your Dream

What will you write?

Biggest and finest dream,

Think for a minute,

This thing is not minute,

On everything you can write,

Believe in your dream,

Conquering that dream,

In a brink of a minute,

Is the best theme to write,

So stand up and write your finest dream in a minute.

Dr. Diwakar Pokhriyal

Chapter – 46
Villanelle Poetry

The Park

In the night so dark,

I set to find the peace,

I sat on the park,

That was so stark,

I was feeling at the crease,

In the night so dark,

In search of a spark,

I found a piece,

I sat on the park,

Suddenly heard a bark,

And voices of trees,

In the night so dark,

New journey I had to embark,

As if I had to pay the fees,

I sat on the park,

Found not even a mark,

Hiding from the bees,

In the night so dark,

I sat on the park.

There's a Poet in Everyone

At the sea

Wandering like a lost bee,

Lost inside demonic passion,

I paused, looking at the silent sea,

Me and my dreams, we flee,

In the thoughts of obsession,

Wandering like a lost bee,

But purity and meaning are free,

Acceptance of catastrophe should be in fashion,

I paused, looking at the silent sea

Thoughts were fishing while sipping the tea,

Heart was afraid of recession,

Wandering like a lost bee,

Well the sophisticated trust in me,

Was still, in the progression,

I paused, looking at the silent sea

Yes, that sea was silent as she,

But, was standing by my side in each session,

Wandering like a lost bee,

I paused, looking at the silent sea.

Chapter – 47
Yadu

Angel and Devil

Silent chaste smile,

Opens file bit slow,

Agile is heart,

Hide in shirt, now,

Like flying in passion, tied with compassion

Hot summer burns,

A Truth churns on,

None learns to care,

Shy to share life,

Lose layers of the true feelings

Both dives deep,

Like a sleeping

And creeping dive,

Short beehive bleeds,

A stride of honey blood totally insane.

There's a Poet in Everyone

Life is a thrill

Life is a thrill,

So just chill out,

To kill the fear,

Shift the gear, fast,

And hear the tone that just lasts

Imbibe in eyes,

All the skies up,

The lies must end,

Start a trend soon,

And lend to self, shining moon

Soak in the fun,

Never run off,

Just stun the smile,

Oh! Cool style, Bro,

The file of life is kept low.

Dr. Diwakar Pokhriyal

Chapter – 48
A Zejel

Comparison

Look at the monk, walking alone,
And poor me with no dial tone,
Engulfed completely by the loan,

I looked around, Goon was behind,
Including me, whole world is blind,
Everyone ahead, me rewind,
Feeling now, as if I am thrown,

And that lone monk wanders in peace,
Poor me, ambitious to touch Greece,
Not able to earn the damn fees,
My mom says 'Your brain has been grown?'

Compact

Minimum words, full of action,
Not bothered with the reaction,
Life is full, we live a fraction

We end up knowingly in hell
Silent whole life, we never yell,
Blind towards truth, ringing same bell,
Gaining insight for attraction,

We need to make our life compact,
Like the mountains, just do not react,
Otherwise, we will lose the tact,
We will lose track in Selection.

Chapter – 49
Alphabet Fever Poetry

Battle battling battle,

(The B fever)

Base breaching Battles

Battle battling battle,

Briskly bouncing broken battle,

Battered blooded battle,

Bumpy boomerangs battle,

Broadly broad battle,

Bad blossoms battle,

Bedridden busty battle,

Blindly brought battle

Breaking betterment battle,

Borrowing blood battle,

Backed by black belt battle,

Bursting Bombshell battle,

Becoming brotherhood battle,

Baseless base battle,

Bringing Brilliance battle,

Bestselling books battle,

Boring bore battle,

Buddy bugging battle,

Brisky baby battle,

Beautiful Bridging battle

Breaking backbone battle
Break-less brick breaking battle,
Boating breathless battle,
Battling bands battle,
Bubbly brotherly battle
Backyard burglar battle,
Birthday bash battle,
Buying burger battle,
Bouncing back Business battle
Boarding bunking battle
Befriending babe battle.

Erroneously Enacted
(The "E" Fever)
Elephant elopes effortlessly,
Evidences emits Excuses
Emergent Eyes erodes,
Emphatic epical epic,
Entertaining eagle-eous eagerness,
Emitting entrant energy,
Envisioning embarking emergence,
Encapsulating enticing exactness,
Ever-ready errant enchants,
Engulfing eroding emptiness,
Ears eludes enlightenment,
Engendering ebb,

Endangered eclipse evolving

Erroneous errors,

Edgy eggs experience,

Emerging emphatic emergency,

Enacting enormously,

End ending endlessly,

Earning envisions Earrings

Eating early evenings

Europe, England, Egypt,

Encrypted exhausted e-mail

Frenetic Fool

(The F fever)

Ferociously furious Fool,

Foul fouled fan,

Fantastic food faltered,

Forgetting fine fineness,

Faulty fever fumes,

Foreigner feeble fort,

Fishy fish finds,

Frenzy frenetic friends,

Flying fly flies

Foggy fortune fries,

Fabulous frame frames,

Fire folded fright,

Frightening fight frowns,

Fully fractured foot,

Finding Fat Face,

Fatty fluky fruit,

Fluttering flattening flat,

Fondling first fret,

Founder founded fragility,

Frog faced Fox,

Finally final frontier,

Fostering fuzziness,

Few from fraternity,

Funny funky flunky,

For free fans

Football floor flooded,

Fact flown family

Faces forbearance facet

Feathery Flip-flop,

Forgets Finest Flock,

Greatest Grudge
(The G fever)

Greatness goes,

Grudge grills,

Genius gene generates,

Generic gruesome genie,

Grudge grizzle goal,

Goat getting gunned,

Grey gray goon,

Gloomy Gift generator,

Goes gelling,

Giggling giggle giggles,

Ground grounding grunts,

Greek grapes geeks,

Ginger gang grumble,

Goofy green glimpse,

Gangster gems,

Grainy glittering greetings,

Ghostly gutter,

Gentleness goes grunting,

Gentle gloving guts

Grammy, granny grooves,

Gumming germs generations,

Grooms greater gangster,

Greatest grudge.

Humanly human
(The H fever)
Humming heated Harmony

Hesitant hear hassles,

How Human handles,

Horizontally hovering handle,

Hottest honey holds,

Hopeless hipster,

There's a Poet in Everyone

Hip hop honeymoon,
Houses helpless homelessness,
Heard hot humiliation,
Hunter humanly hunts
Hitting hit hibernation,
Holding heartless hopes,
Holes haphazardly hues,
Happenings happens honestly,
Halloween hollow hints,
Honesty horrendously hides,
Hidden hammering hammers,
Hazardous harmful hens,
Humbleness humbles hooters,
Hooting heartfelt hurdles,
Higher hump hustling,
Hunting helical helicopter,
Hyperbolic hymn,
Hilly hungry horse,
Harmonic Help hopes,
Hero's heroic host,
Hostage humble hotel,
Helium, halogen, hydrogen.

Insight
(The "I" fever)

I insist in incarnation,

Dr. Diwakar Pokhriyal

In-spite invoicing inside,

Interacting Inhumanely,

Inspecting innocence,

Imbibing innately,

In-sighting Immortality

Instead innumerable in-acts,

Irrationally irked,

Inking invisible ink,

I investigated insights,

Is it implausible?

Immature in-vibes,

Inaccessible ingredients,

Instilled Inactively,

Indicating inception,

In-depth initiation,

Indicating impact,

Impatient invoice,

Ill-mannered ill-fated,

Incessant Illness

Implicating immatureness,

Implicit itchiness,

Is it imparting Innovation?,

Immaterial immaculateness,

Inviolable Images incarnated,

Imagining immersed Inn

Chapter – 50
Freedoetry* (Freedom Poetry)

Decisions

6 lines x 4 paragraphs = 24 syllable in each paragraph

It is you,

To decide about,

Your future,

Hanging in balance,

Either to,

Create history,

Or lost in,

Mystery of,

Shallow words,

Directionless actions,

Or big,

Majority crises,

As in the end,

When you would,

Be all alone,

Sitting on a lone chair,

Either,

You will smile or cry,

Will you have,

A smile,

Of contentment,

Or tears of,

Unmet wishes?

It is now your own decision.

Night

4 lines x 3 paragraphs = 12 syllabus in each paragraph.

Darkness wins,

When light fails,

Stars twinkles,

To ignite,

Pure,

Positivity,

Or,

Negativity,

The decision,

Rests on,

The soul,

That burns in night

Fun road

3 lines *3 paragraphs = 9 syllable each para

Keep running,
In search of fun,
Fun road,

Dancing, singing,
And jabbing,
Endless,

So prepare,
Yourself to fly,
With fun.

Dr. Diwakar Pokhriyal

Chapter – 51
Poetry Rainbow

Keep writing

Never leave the thoughts alone, (free verse)

That is so bad, (cinquain)

Know the truth, (etheree)

Continuity rules here, (Tanka)

Waving the flag so high, (Acrostic)

Instigating inspiration, (Alleteration)

Connecting with that almighty through verses and thoughts. (Fibonacci)

Rest

After a long working hell, (free verse)

I need, (etheree)

A symphonic rest, (senryu)

To rebuild, (fibonacci)

My lost determination, (Tanka)

Rocking righteous rest, (Alliteration)

That will help me in overcoming every test. (rhyme)

Rejection

Rejection is painful, (Acrostic)

Oh, (Fibonacci)

My broken heart cries, (Senryu)

There's a Poet in Everyone

Trying to forget the ties, (Rhyme)

But timeless tears are umpteen, (Tanka)

Ugly, Unwanted, Useless, (Alliteraion)

That is making me realize the pain. (Free Verse)

Greenery

Such wonderful and lively scenery, (Reverse Etheree)

Heart touching flawless greenery, (Couplet)

Needs to be preserved, (Senryu)

From demonic pollution, (Tanka)

From polluted minds, (Fibonacci)

To make this world - "heaven", (Etheree)

Reflecting the existence of humanity. (Acrostic)

Blind Attempts

Bleak first step towards glory, (Acrostic)

A beginning of marvellous story, (Couplet)

Cunningly continues catastrophically, (Alliteration)

Blind attempts, (Fibonacci)

In hope of enlightening, (Tanka)

Faulty Glittering Hopeless, (Abeceradian)

Independence screams aloud. (free verse)

The Students

Twinkling stars painting, (Haiku)

Canvas of that almighty, (Tanka)

History makers, (Senryu)

Ready to follow instructions, (Cinquain)

With pure mind and soul, (Fibonacci)

Resting their belief in those teachers, (Free Verse)

Unaware of politics and preachers. (Rhyming)

Flowers

Do you remember the time? (Free Verse)

Delicate flower blossoms, (Tanka)

Overpowers spring, (Haiku)

Lovers are teased, (Etheree)

Oh My, (Cinquain)

Raining Freshness, (Acrostic)

Beauty all around to harness. (Rhyme)

Teach

Teach me now till death, (Acrostic)

Making me eligible, (Haiku)

To rise, (Fibonacci)

Anytime and anywhere, (Alliteration)

Against the death and darkness, (Tanka)

To understand the strife, (Free Verse)

To search true meaning of life. (Rhyme)

Lovers

Lips are sultry, (Acrostic)

There's a Poet in Everyone

And eyes, sleepy, (Cinquain),
It is Childish love, (Senryu)
Locked hands and open pity, (Tanka)
Spreading disease in whole city, (Rhyme)
Stamping that misunderstanding, (Fibonacci)
Polluting the love so pure. (Etheree)

Battle

Battle of battle, (Acrostic)
Starting, (Etheree)
Right now, (Fibonacci)
Prepare yourself for the attack, (Cinquain)
Against all those evil minds, (Tanka)
To conquer the will, (Reverse Etheree)
And to spread the light. (Free Verse)

Chapter – 52
Heptaoem

Writing

Misunderstood,

By,

Maximum,

Brains,

Yet,

Surviving,

Writing.

Prepare

War,

Ends,

Humanity,

Starts,

Pure,

Hatred,

Prepare

Soft

Torn,

Apart,

Instantaneously,

Laughed,

Off,

Mostly,

Soft.

Fun

Loneliness,

Kills,

Togetherness,

Haunts,

Life,

Rocks,

Fun

Sleep

Essential,

Food,

Human,

Growth,

Requires,

Adequacy,

Sleep.

Dr. Diwakar Pokhriyal

Chapter – 53
Remix Poetry

Ready

(Senryu + Lyrette + Acrostic+ Quatrain + Fibonacci + Enclosed Rhyme + Tanka)

Destruction alone

A new birth of sanity

The lord of humans

Oh Lord!

My pure soul,

Is now ready,

For humanity,

To fight evil,

To protect,

To rise

Rigorous bloody sensations,

Eating away thy soul,

Ardent believe is boiling,

Deadly sighs needs to end,

Yes, I want war,

A war for new beginning of life,

Ending all the tormented tears,

There's a Poet in Everyone

Ending that ultimate strife,
To eradicate all fears,

I,
Want,
To kill,
Pain and mask,
And insanity
To create a world within peace

Oh lord! Give me power,
To clear off this mist of sham,
To clear off this spam,
Oh lord! Drown me in shower,

My believe in truth is intact,
I am aware of my awareness,
Ready to end the darkness,
I am standing to make this pact,

I am screaming loud,
"Come on demon let us fight",
For ultimate prize,
For holy world and the truth,
I am just ready to die.

Dr. Diwakar Pokhriyal

Life is unknown

(Acrostic + Abecarderian + Couplets + Triplets + Alleteration + Enclosed Rhyme + Free verse)

Life is so colourful,
Instigates numerous emotions,
Flaunts the tragedies,
Enlightens the soul,

Atrocious at times,
Bewildering rhymes,

Cauchy thoughts enslaves,
Dusky moments and caves,

Enticing, emphatic at times,
Flabbergasting creative chimes,

Gems are actually rare,
Hate 'the demon' seems so fair,

Invites the troubles easily,
Journey ends, not luckily,

Kneels the heart so often,
Lofty and lousy villain,

There's a Poet in Everyone

Mimicks merciless mountains,

Naughty life, nasty nights, nostalgic terrains,

Omnipotent God unknown,

Pilgrims misunderstands the tone,

Quenching thoughts aren't valid here,

Rustic souls are living in fifth gear,

Shining spring swirls at sun,

Titanic treasures triumps being stun,

Uncanny moments are many,

Validity isn't any,

Wax is the material of nanny,

X-mas isn't ordinary,

Yes, life needs a visionary,

Zooming into the task, as in archery,

Droplets of the blood,

Paints the canvas of our life,

A warrior is born

Life is black like a clouded sky,

Instigating the obvious pain,

Dr. Diwakar Pokhriyal

Installing the teary rain,
Life is at times so shy,

No-one can predict, when,
Which color will shine,
Oh Lord, it's so interesting,
To leave everything on you,
To believe in goodness,
To live every moment, free.

Thoughts

(Acrostic + Senryu + Free Verse + Enclosed Rhyme + Etheree + Cinquian + Nonet)

Tirelessly a circle was drawn,
Having radius of our love,
Oh, the circumference was our hug,
United us beyond time,
Gems were those seconds,
Twinkling in the diameter,
Slowly shifting to the centre,

And the planet dance,
At Divine Possibilty,
Once in a life time,

We neutralized our differences,

There's a Poet in Everyone

As the acid become basic,
The atoms danced with molecules,
We escaped with the gases,
To a world of bodies,
Ameobic shaped creatures,
Oh! We were stunned,
Looking at the evolution,

And when you held me close,
The beatles started to show,
Every note of music, to row,
The moment of love we chose,

Our breath started dancing,
And the heartbeat ran,
No, I had no plan,
But our eyes started romancing,

I,
Was lone,
Spectator,
Of your unmatched,
Treat of lovely love,
Like scoring a death goal,
That was just sensational,
Like an exquisite cover drive,

Dr. Diwakar Pokhriyal

I was lost in the beauty of you,
And you wrapped me into your elation,

And then,
We crossed oceans,
Crossed heavens together,
To become those eternal thoughts,
As one.

We united for once in for all
The hoax of death was scared of us,
The demon of the pain died,
We crucified the time,
Unity painted,
The resurgence,
Of one soul,
Of one,
Love.

Life
(Rhyme + Acrostic + Enclosed Rhyme + Haiku + Etheree + Nonet + English Quintet)

I don't know, exactly,
What is this called 'Life'?
Some painted emotions,
Or the tainted strife,

There's a Poet in Everyone

I don't know exactly,
What is this called 'Life'
Walking through, bed of roses,
Or at the edge of knife,

Lament over the stars,
Intriguing and innate,
Frisking and fatal,
Energetic and enchanting,

I don't know, the point,
How should I rate,
Or am I just late?,
I don't know, the joint,

Life might become a rainbow,
Piercing drops of heart,
Alas, eradication of dirt,
Is but Oh God, so slow,

Winter of heaven,
The crux of life is unknown,
A walking zombie,

Life,
Is just,

Dr. Diwakar Pokhriyal

Like the cards,
Packed in the box,
Waiting to show us,
Their true worth in the game,
But are we really smart,
Picking the right card, the right time,
Or Alas, we are just trying, and,
Are trying to pretend that winning smile

All those soaring clouds defines the life,
Emotive droplets, hidden sighs,
Felicitating nature,
Those blind and deaf creatures,
Are the synonyms,
For, so called Life,
We are still,
Feeding,
Lies,

No matter what we say,
Life is still unknown,
No matter how we stay,
We make our canvas alone,
Carving on the mud or stone.

There's a Poet in Everyone

My love

(Enclosed rhyme + Etheree + Lyrette + Rhyme + Fibonacci + Acrostic + Quintet)

I remember our meeting,

When you were wetted by rain,

No sign of tears or pain,

I still felt like cheating,

How can that dropping drop,

Touch your rosy lips,

You were the cause of slips,

You were my only crop,

That

Rainbow,

Of our love,

Of our cozy,

And passionate hug,

And you beautiful eyes,

Melted my sighs into you,

And your fiery breath was heating,

My desires of closeness and freedom,

For a heaven of love and care of souls,

Pure love,

Natural,

Dr. Diwakar Pokhriyal

And breathtaking,
And your timeless touch
Digs so deep down,
To cherish,
To live,

And when I kissed the drops,
Resting on your cheeks,
I felt inside my heart,
Elation of numerous winning streaks,

Oh my queen you wet hair,
Were touching my neck,
Our ship of love was sailing,
Without the fear of being wreck,

Oh,
Love,
You are,
My angel,
Your sublime kisses,
Evokes life inside dead desires

Majestic tightness of your hug,
Youthful passion was on,

There's a Poet in Everyone

Love was painting the clock,

Overwhelmed senses went greedy,

Vivacious sun of adore,

Enchanted the symphony of trust,

Oh my queen of heart,

How can I forget our meeting,

My senses were slave of your flirt,

And my fortune was shining with our dating,

My memories still have your fragrance and every second it is elating.

Dr. Diwakar Pokhriyal

Chapter – 54
Zig Zag Rhyming

Around the world

Raise your awareness,

Harness the hope and chase,

Base is to be built to impress,

Cess is high for the trace,

Know the world around,

Sound of air and snow,

Low and lost or found,

Bound self, you won't grow,

Prime in the perspective of you,

Clue? Go around with rhyme,

Crime shouldn't stop the dew,

New, will be your world with time.

Chapter – 55
Encryptive Poetry

Encryptive Poetry - 1

Bharat Chants Green, in it's teen,

Tamed odor, two Webbed Jean,

Kate is Kate, Know matter, eighteen,

Uttering kept low, Apple helps you mean?

Moon is odd Saviour, Larger than life's dean,

Keep offering assurance, Man, this girl is mean.

The Hidden Message is 'INDIAN CLASSICAL DANCE FORMS AND THEIR ORIGIN'

ODD LINES = Dance Forms

EVEN LINES = their Origin

Line – 1

Bharat - Bharatnatyam

Ch – Chhau

Gr - Gaudiya Nritya

Line – 2

Ta - Tamil Nadu (origin of Bharatnatyam)

OD - Odisa (origin of Chhau)

Two WEB - West Bengal , West Bengal (origin of Chhau & Gaudiya)

Jh - Jharkhand (origin of Chhau)

Line – 3

Ka - Kathak

Ka - Kathakali

K- Kuchipudi

Ma - Manipuri

Line 4

UTT - Uttar Pradesh (origin of Kathak)

Ke - Kerla (origin of Kathakali)

Ap - Andhra Pradesh (origin of Kuchipudi)

Mean - Manipur ((origin of Manipuri)

Line 5

Mo – Mohiniyattam

Od – odissi

Sa – Sattriya

Than - Thang Ta

Line 6

Ke - Kerla (origin of Mohiniyattam)

Ord - Odisa (origin of odissi)

As - Assam (origin of Sattriya)

Man - Manipur (origin of Thang Ta)

There's a Poet in Everyone

Encryptive Poetry - 2

Ashu Became Bold, Dog gulped at hold,

Waka Waka sold, Knot, male or mold,

Main mark was told, Net picked was old,

Put my Sap and Siren, Tale tempts U to hold.

The Hidden Message is 'Official Languages of India' (Words used for the message are in Alphabetical order)

Line 1

AS - Assamese,

BE - Bengali,

BO - Bodo,

DO - Dogri,

GU- Gujraati,

H- Hindi,

Line-2

KA - Kannada,

KA - Kashmiri,

KNO - Konkani,

MA - Manipuri,

M - Malyalam,

Line-3

MAI - Maithili,

MAR - Marathi,

NE - Nepali,

O -Odia,

Line-4

PU - Punjabi,

SA - Sanskrit,

SI - Sindhi,

TA - Tamil,

TE - Telgu,

U – Urdu

Encryptive Poetry - 3

Petal in Jan, Matter in Van, Ban the Love, National plan

Lion capital of Ashoka clan, Ganga rows, dolphin ran.

The Hidden Message 'National Bird, Animal, Anthem, Song, Fruit, Flower, Tree, Emblem, river and aquatic animal of INDIA'

Line - 1

PE - National Bird – Peacock

T - National Animal – Tiger

JAN - National Anthem - Jan gan

MA - National Fruit – Mango

VA - National song – Vande Maatram,

BA - Nation Tree.. Banyan

LO - National Flower – Lotus

Line -2

Lion Capital of Ashoka - National Emblem - Lion Capital of Ashoka at Sarnath

Ganga - National River - Ganga

Dolphin - National Aquatic Animal - Dolphin.

Encryptive Poetry - 4

An Apple Asked Bijoy, Chew Chew Dam Die?,

Deep Gulp or Goat, Hate, Hope & Joy,

Jammy Kate & kettle, Lamp, 'Maddy & Macoy',

Man 'T' missed the meet, Nah, odd pun was coy,

Race stumped him Dry, Tempting Task or troy, Utopia of Uttering Why?

The Hidden Encryption is - 'The names of States & UT of INDIA'

Line 1

An - Andaman Nicobar

App – AP and AP ...Andhra Pradesh and Arunachal Pradesh

As – Assam

Bi --- Bihar

Ch – Chandigarh

Ch- Chattisgarh

Dam Die – Dadra and Nagar Haveli , Daman & Diu,

Line – 2

De – Delhi

Gu – Gujrat

Goa – Goa

Ha – Haryana

Hop - Himachal Pradesh

J - Jharkhand

Line – 3

Jam – J and K

Ka – Karnatka

Ke – Kerla

La – Lakshdeep

Mad - Madhya Pradesh

Ma – Maharastra

Line – 4

Man I – Manipur

Mis – Mizoram

Me – Meghalya

Na – Nagaland

O – Orissa

Pun- Punjab & Puducherry

Line-5

Ra – Rajasthan,

There's a Poet in Everyone

S – Sikkim,

Te – Telangna,

Ta – Tamilnadu ,

Tr – Tiipura,

U - Uttar Pradesh,

Utt- Uttranchal,

W – West Bengal

Dr. Diwakar Pokhriyal

About The Author

Dr. Diwakar Pokhriyal has completed his PhD, Post-Graduation and B. Tech in Power/Energy. He is a writer by passion. He has written 14 poetry books, 2 short story collection and 1 Novel. He has been a part of more than 100 poetry anthologies/magazines with writers around the world. He has won 'India Start Icon Award 2019' for his book Poetry for Everyone. He has also been listed into 'Top 50 Influencer Author's Award 2K18' by The Spirit Mania. His name is also in 'Limca Book of Records – 2017' for writing most varieties of poem. He has won "Aagaman Young Talent - 2015" award for his writing endeavors. He has won "Poiesis Award for Excellence in Literature-2014 & 2017" for his short stories. He has been a highly recommended poet in an international competition "Rabindranath Tagore Award – 2016" by xpresspublication.com. His works and interviews are also included in various websites.

Facebook Page: Poetry For Everyone
Twitter Handle: @poetofsenses
Email: pokhriyal_diwakar@yahoo.com
Youtube Channel: Creative Energy

www.ingramcontent.com/pod-product-compliance
Lightning Source LLC
Chambersburg PA
CBHW031346040426
42444CB00005B/209